TEACH YOURSELF

HT...

Publishing on the World Wide Web

Second Edition

Mac Bride

Hodder & Stoughton

A MEMBER OF THE HODDER HEADLINE GROUP

For UK orders: please contact Bookpoint Ltd, 39 Milton Park, Abingdon, Oxon OX14 4TD. Telephone: (44) 01235 400414, Fax: (44) 01235 400454. Lines are open from 9.00 – 6.00, Monday to Saturday, with a 24 hour message answering service. Email address: orders@bookpoint.co.uk

For U.S.A. & Canada orders: please contact NTC/Contemporary Publishing, 4255 West Touhy Avenue, Lincolnwood, Illinois 60646 – 1975 U.S.A. Telephone: (847) 679 5500, Fax: (847) 679 2494.

Long renowned as the authoritative source for self-guided learning – with more than 30 million copies sold worldwide – the *Teach Yourself* series includes over 200 titles in the fields of languages, crafts, hobbies, sports, and other leisure activities.

British Library Cataloguing in Publication Data
A catalogue record for this title is available from The British Library

Library of Congress Catalog Card Number: On file

First published in UK 1996 by Hodder Headline Plc, 338 Euston Road, London NW1 3BH.

First published in US 1998 by NTC/Contemporary Publishing, 4255 West Touhy Avenue, Lincolnwood (Chicago), Illinois 60646 – 1975 U.S.A.

The 'Teach Yourself' name and logo are registered trade marks of Hodder & Stoughton Ltd.

🍄 Typeset by MacDesign, Southampton.
Printed in Great Britain for Hodder & Stoughton Educational, a division of Hodder Headline Plc, 338 Euston Road, London NW1 3BH by Cox & Wyman Ltd, Reading, Berkshire.

First published 1996
Second edition published 1998

Impression number	12	11	10	9	8	7	6	5
Year		2004	2003	2002	2001	2000	1999	

──CONTENTS──

PREFACE

I'll let you into a secret – *HTML (HyperText Markup Language) is simple*. Its vocabulary contains no more than a few dozen words, and its syntax is clear and logical. You can master enough HTML in a few hours to be able to create a basic Web page, and in only a few days to create far more complex ones. And it doesn't get harder as you get further into it – some of the most impressive effects require only the simplest code. Having said that, don't think you will be able to knock up a brilliant Web page in a matter of minutes. Good pages need a lot of thought put into their design, and a lot of time put into their implementation.

I have written this book mainly for home users who want to develop their own home pages, and for small businesses who would like to use the Web to advertise their products and services. It won't show you how to sell over the Web – that raises a host of legal and security issues that could not be fitted into these 224 pages.

This second edition has been extended to cover the HTML editors in the new Netscape and Explorer browsers, and to give an introduction to the use of animated images, applets and other enhancements for Web pages. I have also taken the opportunity to pick up some issues raised by readers of the first edition. Keep the feedback coming!

mailto:macbride@tcp.co.uk

http://www.tcp.co.uk/~macbride/tybooks

September 1997

ACKNOWLEDGEMENTS

Level 9 Software – *for Ingrid Bottomlow and scenes from the Dribble Valley;*

Total Connectivity Providers – *for the provision of Web space, and all-the-year-round good service;*

Named and unnamed contributors to the World Wide Web – *for the screens I have captured, and the help and inspiration I have gleaned.*

1

HOME PAGES

1.1 Aims of this chapter

The main purpose of this chapter is to get you thinking about what you might like to publish on the World Wide Web. We will take a first brief look at the nature of HTML and how it relates to the Web, then examine some of the ideas behind home pages and see what some other people have done with theirs.

1.2 HTML

HTML stands for HyperText Markup Language, and is the means by which Web pages are created and linked together. It developed from SGML (Standardised General Markup Language), and if you want to know any more about SGML, look on the Web at:

http://www.ncrel.org/~rtilmann/htmltools.html

This is a practical book, not a history book.

HTML is based on the use of tags. These are key words or phrases, enclosed in <angle brackets>, which describe how text and graphics are to be displayed, and create links between different documents or parts of the same document. It is HTML's ability to handle links that makes the Web possible. The World Wide Web is essentially an ever-expanding set of interlinked HTML documents, and a Web browser, like Netscape, is essentially a tool that can display these documents and follow up the links embedded in them.

HTML is continually under development, alongside the browsers that read it. HTML 2.0 is the base line. Netscape 1.1 introduced extensions to this, and most were absorbed into HTML 3.0. Netscape 2.0 added new facilities, which have gained general acceptance. Further extensions to HTML have been introduced by Netscape 3.0 and Communicator, and by Microsoft's Internet Explorer 4.0. Microsoft and Netscape have yet to accept each other's developments as standard!

Mosaic, and early versions of Netscape and Internet Explorer will cope with almost everything in the first half of the book. Internet Explorer 3.0 and 4.0 should also be able to handle most of the later examples, but Netscape 3.0 or Communicator is recommended. How often have you come across 'This page looks best in Netscape' messages when browsing the Web?

Where a tag or option is not supported by HTML 2.0, it will be flagged:

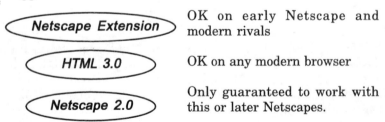

Netscape Extension — OK on early Netscape and modern rivals

HTML 3.0 — OK on any modern browser

Netscape 2.0 — Only guaranteed to work with this or later Netscapes.

——— 1.3 What is a home page? ———

A 'home page' may refer to a simple one-page document belonging to an individual user, or to the point of entry into a huge site run by a multinational corporation. It may fit into a single screen, or may be so long that it fills 10 or 20 screens. It may be consist of a single text file, or may have dozens of graphics, video and sound clips and other items embedded in it.

If you want to have a home page, it must be stored on a computer that other users can access. For big businesses, this means a machine that has been set up to allow two-way traffic; for individuals and smaller businesses, this means on their Internet access provider's machine. Most providers now offer free Web storage space to their personal members, and cheap space to their business users.

YOUR WEB SPACE

Check that your Internet access provider can offer you Web space. If they do not offer this service, change your provider now! And if you are shopping around, check how much space they will let you use free – some are significantly more generous than others. You may not have great ambitions as a Web publisher, but it's always good not to have to worry too much about limitations.

Personal home pages

So here you are, with Web space at your disposal, a desire for world-wide publicity, and two questions on your lips. What do I put on my home page? How do I do it? Both are rather large questions. I'll tackle the first one now, then take the rest of the book over the second.

— 1.4 What goes on a home page? —

There are two aspects to this. What is the message that you are trying to get across? What mixture of text, graphics, forms, tables and links to other files and pages will best achieve that aim?

The message

If you are running a business, the obvious answer is to use your home page for advertising, and perhaps marketing your products and services. (Telling people about your products is straightforward, selling them over the Internet raises problems that are not tackled in this book.)

The home page for Computer Bookshops – go there and buy another of my books on-line!

If you are the secretary or publicist for a club or society, the home page can be used to inform members – and prospective members – about its activities. It can also be used to gather feedback from members.

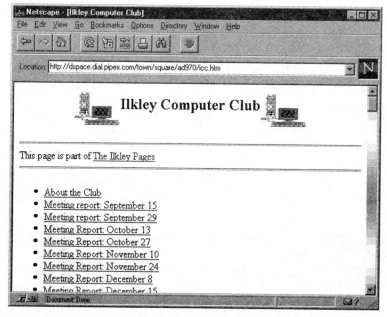

An example of a simple, but effective home page for a club. The links at the top act as a 'Contents' list for the page. Clicking on one of these takes you down the page to the chosen report.

If you have a particular hobby or interest that you would like to share with others, you could turn your page into an information centre for that topic. If are a fan of a star, a group, a writer or a TV show, set up a fanzine on your page. You do not have to be an expert to do this – just an enthusiast. Spend time researching the Internet and gathering together links to information and other resources. Make your page a prime jumping-off point for your subject, let everyone know that it is there and you will earn the appreciation – and perhaps the friendship – of fellow enthusiasts from around the world.

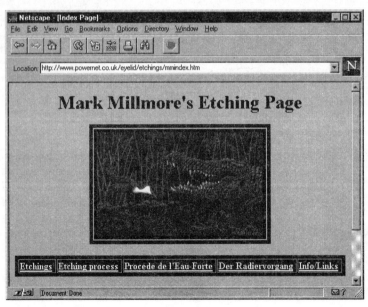

If you are a poet, musician, writer, artist or photographer, you can use your home page as a showcase for your works. (I don't think it is worth putting a novel or symphony on your page, as I can't see many people bothering to wait while it downloads.)

The one thing that is not a very good idea, is to use your home page solely to tell the world about yourself. Unless you are a celebrity, very few people will be interested in you. Sorry to break this news to you, but it is as well to know before you start to design your page.

Come to think of it, will anybody be really interested in you, even if you are a celebrity?

Opposite

Two good examples of home pages where the authors are providing useful links to other pages or information about their personal or professional interests.

The content

Text

Text is good. Text travels quickly over the Net. And it doesn't have to look boring. You have lots of control over the size of the characters, and of the placing and alignment of text. You can even choose its colour.

Text is also easy to handle. You can lay out a page of neatly formatted text, with several levels of headings and ruled lines between sections, using only a limited set of very simple tags. With a little effort and a couple more tags, you can create bulleted or numbered lists of items. These aspects of text are all covered in Chapters 2 and 6.

If you are feeling adventurous, you can move on from lines of text, to text in tables. These can be a very attractive way to display organised information, though they are rather fiddly to set up – every part of the heading, every row and every item in the table needs its own tag! We will leave these alone until Chapter 8, and deal with the easier stuff first.

Graphics

They say 'a picture is worth a thousand words.' If you think in terms of downloading time, it would be better to say 'a picture takes as long as several thousand words'. The picture here (250 x 400 pixels), stored as a JPG file – the most compact format – takes 25Kb, which is enough for over 1,500 words – or about 10 full screens of text. Depending upon the baud rate of your modem and the amount of traffic to a site, it takes anything from 10 to 40 seconds to download this much data.

If you are going to include graphics in your page, they must be either (a) worth seeing, or (b) tiny. People can get very irritated if they have to wait 2 or 3 minutes, only to find that they have downloaded an out-of-focus picture of your pet rabbit, or your firm's boring logo. The crocodile image on the etching page, for example, was around 14Kb – quite small, and certainly worth waiting for. Jeremy Beadle's photograph took 8Kb – at least it was small. Look again at Beadle's home page. There are three other images visible on that screen. The top heading and the 'Wanted' are graphics, not text, and another graphic is used to create the background. These are all small – no more than 2Kb – but give a lot of impact to the page.

You will see how to add graphics in Chapter 3.

Some people include **multimedia** clips in their home pages, though the arguments about quality and download time apply to these, even more than they do to still graphics. You don't get many seconds of video in a Megabyte, and it can take longer to download an audio clip than to listen to it! All access providers set limits to your Web storage space, and one multimedia clip could well push you up against – or beyond – the limits of your free space.

There is another point to be borne in mind. With video and audio files, your visitors must have suitable software to view or hear them, and for both types there are a number of different formats. Whichever format you choose, there is no guarantee that your visitors will be able to view the clips.

Multimedia clips are covered in Chapter 4.

Counters are a neat idea, and fairly easy to implement. Add one to record the number of visitors to your site. It is an effective way to assess how much interest your page is generating. You can see one in the illustration on page 12. The Top 20 – an excellent shareware site – clocked up over 30,000 visitors within a few weeks of starting their counter.

Cool links

No home page is complete without links to other pages – direct
your visitors to your favourite sites, or to the good stuff that you
have found on the Web. They will appreciate the links – with so
many millions of pages on the Web, any pointers towards the
best are always useful. Some people's home pages consist of little
but links, and these pages can be highly valued by other users.

You will see how to create links in Chapter 4.

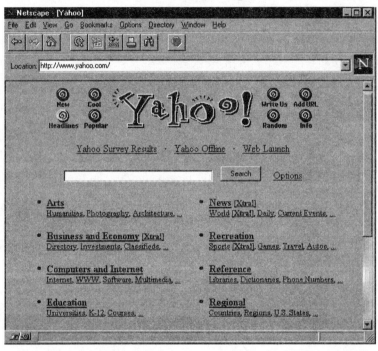

*Yahoo started as the home page of a couple of students. It was one
of the first Internet directories and is now probably the best. Yahoo is
the first place that I look when I am hunting for something new. If you
haven't found it yet, do so now. The URL is: www.yahoo.com. (See
page 68 for an explanation of URLs.)*

Forms

If you want to get feedback from your home page, the best way is to use a form. This consists of a set of slots into which your visitors can write their names and addresses, or whatever other information you seek. If you are in business, a form could collect details from potential customers. If you are running your page as a fan club or enthusiasts' information centre, a form will provide a simple means for fellow enthusiasts to contact you.

As a form is only a set of tags, with a little text, it adds little to the size or download time of a page, however, it does require the active involvement of your access provider. They must run software to collect data submitted by your visitors and pass it on to you. Most providers do this, but if feedback is going to be important to you, check that yours does – now.

We will look at forms in Chapter 7.

Frames, image maps and applets

With **frames** you can divide your page into a set of separate areas, each of which can display a different file and be changed independently. They can greatly improve the look and the usability of your page, but involve a number of complexities. We'll leave those until Chapter 9.

Image maps – larger pictures with several links embedded within them – are increasingly used to act as 'Contents' lists at the top page of sites. Image maps are not hard to create, as you will see in Chapter 10.

Java applets are little programs that can be embedded into pages, to be downloaded and run on within your visitors' browsers. There are several sites on the World Wide Web where you can pick up ready-made applets to slot into your own pages. When you have got your pages up and running, you might like to take time to experiment with these. See Chapter 11 for more on these and other ways of enlivening your pages. And if you want to know more about Java, try *Teach Yourself Java*.

This page has been divided into three frames – one for links to the files, one for the main titles and one for links to the authors.
The main title frame contains a Java applet that scrolls a banner.
Top 20 is run by a group of Web enthusiasts and offers links to the 20 most popular applications for Internet work.
Find it at: **http://www.pi.net/~tuur**

WHERE DID IT GO?

All the sites featured in this book were there when I was writing about them, but unfortunately that's no guarantee that they will still be there when you read about them! Companies and other large organisations tend to stay in one place, but pages run by individuals are likely to move or disappear.

There is a list of updated links on my site at: http:// www.tcp.co.uk/~macbride/tybooks. If you come across any changed links, that are not listed there, let me know.

——— 1.5 Tools for the job ———

You do not need any special software to create simple HTML documents. They can be written on any word-processor or text editor – I normally use Notepad, which does all that is necessary yet takes up little memory. All that is essential is that the software can output plain ASCII text files.

The formatted result can be viewed on your browser, using its Open File command. If your browser is set up so that it goes to your Home page or other Web location on start up, it may be worth changing this while you are developing your HTML files.

Netscape can be set to start on a 'blank page', which stops it from trying to go on-line when the program starts.

To change this setting in *Netscape*, open the **Options** menu and select **General Preferences**.

Select General Preferences on the Options menu

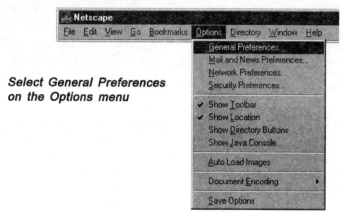

Click on the **Appearance** tab and in the **Start up** options, select **Start with Blank page**.

In earlier versions of Netscape, open the **Options** menu and select **Preferences**. Click on the **Style** tab and set the **Start with Blank page** option there.

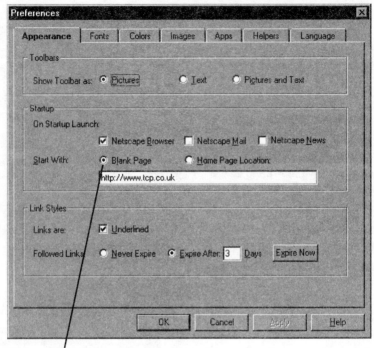

Set it to Start with a Blank page.

There does not seem to be any way to stop Internet Explorer from trying to go on-line. When this starts up, just click *Cancel* when it runs the dial-up software.

WINSOCK OFF-LINE

If you are using Trumpet Winsock for your Internet connection, you may find that your browser will not open unless Winsock is already running. In this case, start Winsock, but do not login, then start the browser.

If you want to include graphics on your page, you should have software that can produce either GIF or JPG files. These are the two most widely used formats – all browsers can display them, and they store images very compactly. Suitable graphics packages are covered in Chapter 3.

When you have created your pages, you will need to upload them to the computer at your service provider – unless you intend to run your own computer as a fully-fledged Web site, which creates all sorts of problems not covered in this book. Uploading is best done with an FTP package – software designed for transferring files in either direction. WS_FTP is the standard Winsock software for this. If you do not have a copy, get one from your service provider.

There are a number of freeware, shareware or commercial HTML editors available. These can cut out some of the donkey work of creating a page, by letting you select formatting controls from menus, rather than typing in the tags directly. A few go even further and offer ready-made templates into which you can drop your own text and images. We will have a look at HTML editors in Chapter 12.

——— 1.6 Learn while you surf ———

Sometimes you will come across a Web page that makes you say 'This is great! How did they do it?' If you really want to know, you can find out easily enough.

Every Web page has two aspects – the display you see on the screen, and the HTML document that created it. Both are accessible from your browser. In Netscape, the command **View|Document Source** (i.e. open the **View** menu and select **Document Source**) will display the original HTML document, or you can use **File|Save As...** to save the document as a text file. Internet Explorer likewise has **View|Source** and **File| Save as File** commands.

```
Netscape - [Source of: file:///C|/Homepage/index.htm]        _ □ ×

<html>

<head>
<title>
Mac's Home Page
</title>
</head>
<body>
<BODY BACKGROUND = "stars.gif" text = "#fff000">
<FONT SIZE = 8>
Welcome to my <FONT SIZE = 8>h<FONT SIZE = 7>u<FONT SIZE = 6>m
<hr>
<FONT SIZE = 5>
<p>Disclaimer:<FONT SIZE = 4> This page is active, mainly so t
<p>You are more than welcome to browse, but don't expect too m
<p>
<FONT SIZE = 6>
<A HREF = author.htm><IMG  Align=Bottom SRC="mac1.gif">Mac</A>
<p>
<hr>
</FONT>
<br>
<FONT SIZE = 6>
Commercial Break
<FONT SIZE = 5>
<p>
<A HREF = inetbks.htm>Books on the Internet </A>by yours truly
<br>
<hr>
<p>
<Font size = 4>
<hr>
<A NAME = links>
Here are some of my favourite links. </A>
<p>
There are 50,000 files at the <A HREF=http://www.jumbo.com> Ju
```

My home page – at an early stage in its development – when viewed as the Document Source in Netscape. What you cannot see here is that different parts of the code are displayed in different colours to make it easier to read. Tags are shown in purple, options in bold with their values in blue, and ordinary text in plain black.

When you are starting with HTML, you may find that other people's documents do not make much sense. Generally speaking, they were written to be viewed, not read, and the authors have not bothered to add notes, or set out the code in a digestible form. However, it will all become clearer in time.

Note that the saved files will not include any of the images, and looking back on them later, you may have difficulty relating the document to the display. If you want to keep the display for later reference, use the PrintScreen key to copy the screen to the Clipboard, then Edit | Paste it into Paint and save that as a file. You can then switch from one to another to compare the document and the display.

1.7 Summary

- An HTML document is a mixture of plain text and tags, which handle links to other pages, graphics, multimedia clips and other enhancements.

- If your service provider does not offer free Web space, find yourself a new provider.

- Spend time thinking about what to put on your home page. If you want people to visit, then there should be something there that they want to see.

- Apart from your browser and a word-processor, you will need FTP software, and a graphics package would be useful. An HTML editor is not necessary, especially not at first.

- You can view the source code for any page on the Web, if you want to see how an effect has been achieved.

2

TEXT AND TAGS

2.1 Aims of this chapter

This chapter introduces the tags that are used to define HTML documents and to format text, using headings, different font sizes and lists of items. It will also take you through the process of creating an HTML file, and viewing it through a browser to check the result.

2.2 HTML tags

Tags are instructions to browsers, telling them how to lay out text, what graphics to display where, what distant pages to link to, and a variety of other things.

Some tags are very simple:

```
<H1>
```

says, 'the next bit of text is to be styled as a level 1 Heading' – i.e. use big type.

Some are much more complex:

```
<IMG SRC = "/images/tiddles.gif" ALT = "My cat" WIDTH = 200
HEIGHT = 100 BORDER = 0 HSPACE = 50 ALIGN = left>
```

This tells the browser which picture to display, where and how big to display it, and what text to use instead, if the visitor chooses not to download the graphic.

A few basic rules are common to all:

- Each tag must be enclosed in <angle brackets>.
- You can use lower or upper case letters. These all have exactly the same effect:

  ```
  <title>
  ```
  ```
  <Title>
  ```
  ```
  <TITLE>
  ```

  Upper case makes them stand out better from the surrounding text. This can be useful, especially when you are checking through the document to find out why the formatting didn't work properly.

- Most tags come in pairs – one to mark the start of a style, the other to mark its end. The tags in each pair are identical, or the closing tag is a simplified version of the opener, except that the closing tag starts with a / forward slash. e.g.

  ```
  <H1>This is a heading</H1>
  ```

- Browsers ignore any spaces or new lines around tags. However, the HTML code will be easier to read if you put spaces around tags, or write them on separate lines. That last example would have been displayed the same on screen if it had been written:

  ```
  <H1>   This is a heading   </H1>
  ```
  or
  ```
  <H1>
  ```
  ```
  This is a heading
  ```
  ```
  </H1>
  ```

—— 2.3 Your first HTML document ——

Run Notepad, or your favourite word-processor, and start up your browser, but do not go on-line. For the time being, keep the documents on your own computer, and view them with the Open File command.

Create a new directory (or Folder in Windows-95-speak) for your HTML files. This is not essential, but if you keep them all together, you won't waste time hunting for them next time.

<HTML>

Every HTML document starts with the tag:

    <HTML>

and ends with:

    </HTML>

So, at its very simplest, an HTML document might read:

    <HTML>
    This is HTML
    </HTML>

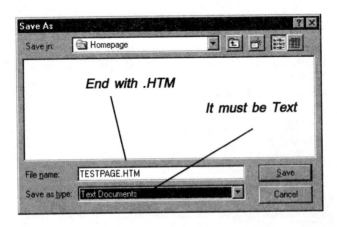

Type this into your word-processor and save it as a Text file, but with the extension .HTM, e.g. *testpage.htm*.

Switch into your browser, use its Open File command and load in your first HTML document. It should look like this.

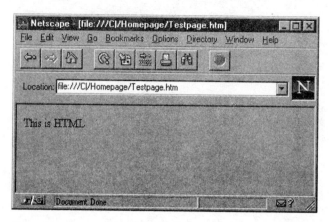

2.4 Headings

There are a set of tags that can be used to define headings over a range of sizes. They all start **<H...** followed by a number between 1 and 6.

Type this into your HTML document, save it and open the file with your browser.

```
<HTML>
<H1> Heading 1 - 24 Point </H1>
<H2> Heading 2 - 18 Point </H2>
<H3> Heading 3 - 14 Point </H3>
<H4> Heading 4 - 12 Point </H4>
<H5> Heading 5 - 10 Point </H5>
<H6> Heading 6 - 7 Point </H6>
Normal body text - 12 Point
</HTML>
```

The resulting display should be something like this.

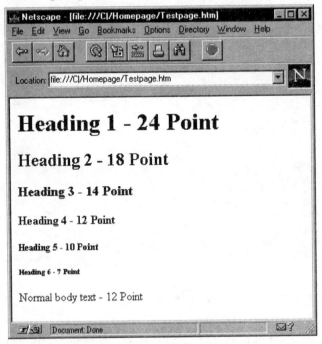

Displays vary because the font is determined by the browser, and this can be changed by the user. How you see your file is not necessarily how other people will see it. Unless they have set their browser up very oddly, an <H1> heading will always be bigger than an <H2>, and so on down the line.

TIME-SAVING TIP

If you are testing out tags, and don't want to keep a permanent copy of the document, do a simple Save after editing, so that the file keeps the same name. When you switch into your browser, rather than going through the **Open File** routine, you can simply hit the **Reload** button.

<TITLE>

Every page should have a title. This is not the text that appears at the top of the page – you do that with a <H1> tag. The title is what appears on the title line of the browser window, and what would be used as a bookmark if anyone bookmarked your page.

It is used in the standard way:

```
<TITLE>
My Home Page
</TITLE>
```

Edit your HTML test document, or set up a new one, to try out the <TITLE> and <H...> tags. Something like this – but with your own text. Including a disclaimer 'This page is under construction' is common practice – it helps to fend off criticism!

<ADDRESS> </ADDRESS>

These tags have a double effect, setting the text into italic and placing it on a new line. The convention is to use these tags only with your e-mail address. That would normally go at the bottom of your home page.

Note the blank lines between sections. They are not necessary – the browser ignores them when it displays the document – but they do make it easier for you to read.

```
<HTML>

<TITLE>
Mac's Home Page
</TITLE>
<H1>Welcome to my Home </H1>
This page is under construction.
<ADDRESS>
macbride@tcp.co.uk
</ADDRESS>

</HTML>
```

Save the document, open it in your browser, and look at it carefully. If it does not show the title, heading and body text as it should, go back to your word-processor file and check that each tag is properly <bracketed> and has its /closing equivalent.

Title **H1 heading** **Body text**

Address

HEAD and BODY

An HTML document can be divided into two parts: the head, enclosed by <HEAD> and </HEAD> contains the title plus any annotations you want to include, but not display; the body, enclosed by <BODY> and </BODY>, is the displayed page. The <BODY> tag can include options to change the colours of the display (see section 2.8).

—— 2.5 Paragraphs and breaks ——

When a browser reads the text in an HTML document, it ignores all excess spaces (only ever displaying one between words), tabs and carriage returns ([Enter] keypresses).

<H...> headings will be placed on separate lines, but if you want to break blocks of body text into paragraphs, or even just start a new line, you have to use one of these three tags.

This is a line BReak and marks the start of a new line.

> Mary had a little lamb
>
> Its fleece was white as snow

will come out as:

> Mary had a little lambIts fleece was white as snow

To get separate lines you must use

> Mary had a little lamb
>
>
>
> Its fleece was white as snow

Note that <BR> stands alone – there is no closing tag.

<P>

This marks the start of a new paragraph, and places a blank line before it. You can equally well place it at the end of a piece of text, at the start of the next, or in between. <P> can be used as a second stand-alone tag, or with a closing </P>.

<HR>

HR stands for Horizontal Rule. This third stand-alone tag separates paragraphs by drawing a line between them. The basic line will be thin, with a shaded effect, and extend almost the full width of the window. This can be changed, see section 6.6.

You can see these three tags at work in the next example.
Substitute your own text, but follow the pattern of tags.

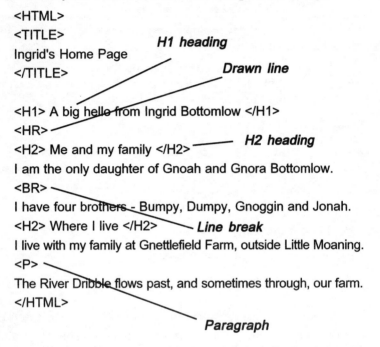

```
<HTML>
<TITLE>
Ingrid's Home Page                    H1 heading
</TITLE>
                                        Drawn line

<H1> A big hello from Ingrid Bottomlow </H1>
<HR>
<H2> Me and my family </H2>             H2 heading
I am the only daughter of Gnoah and Gnora Bottomlow.
<BR>
I have four brothers - Bumpy, Dumpy, Gnoggin and Jonah.
<H2> Where I live </H2>        Line break
I live with my family at Gnettlefield Farm, outside Little Moaning.
<P>
The River Dribble flows past, and sometimes through, our farm.
</HTML>
                                        Paragraph
```

DESIGN WITH TEXT

With 6 levels of headings, paragraph and line breaks, you
have enough to be able to produce clear, well-formatted text.
Experiment and see if this is enough to be able to get your
message across adequately. If it is, you can skip to Chapter
5 and put your Home page on the Web. If you want more
variety in your text, or you would like to include graphics or
links to other pages, then curb your desire to be published,
and read on.

Ingrid's page looks like this. She is exempt from the don't-just-write-about-yourself rule as she is a celebrity – at least to those who remember Level 9 games.

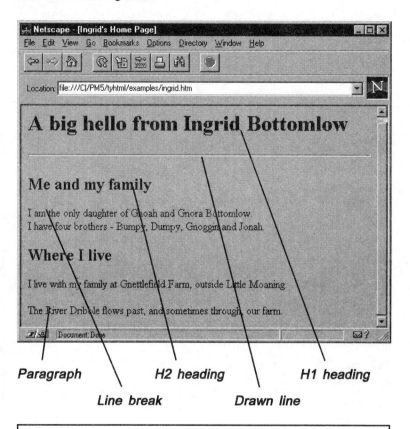

Paragraph

Line break

H2 heading

Drawn line

H1 heading

WORD WRAP

Text is formatted to suit the size of the browser window, with long lines wrapping round at the right edge. If you change the size of the window, the text is automatically reformatted to fit the new width.

—— 2.6 Further text formatting ——

<FONT SIZE = value> ⟨ Netscape Extension ⟩

The <H...> tags are a simple but effective way of creating
headings, but if you want more control over the size of heading
text, or want to vary the size of text *within* a paragraph, you
must use the <FONT SIZE = ... > tag.

The SIZE value can be from 7 down to 2, with 7 being the largest
size, at 36 points. Note that the values run in the opposite
direction to headings, where <H1> is the largest.

FONT SIZE	Heading	Point size
7	–	36 pt
6	<H1>	24 pt
5	<H2>	18 pt
4	<H4>	12 pt bold
3	Body text	12 pt plain
2	–	9 pt

For headings, it is simpler to use the <H...> tags – unless you
want a huge 36 point heading. Keep the <FONT SIZE = ... > tag
for special effects.

To turn off a font size, either set a new <FONT SIZE = ...> or
use </FONT> to revert to the previous size.

Try this:

```
<HTML>
<FONT SIZE = 4> A big <FONT SIZE = 7> Hello </FONT>
from me
</HTML>
```

*This resets the size to the last used. Here it
has the same effect as <FONT SIZE = 4>*

The HTML code opposite produces this 'big Hello'. I haven't included the code for the 'roller coaster ride' shown here. You can work it out. All you need to do is put a new <FONT SIZE = ... > before every letter!

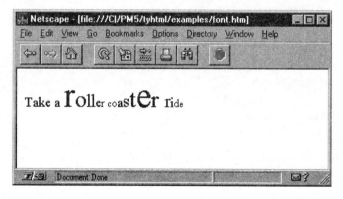

FONTS FALL FLAT

Visitors viewing your page from a browser that can't handle the Netscape FONT SIZE facility, will see plain body text, so your best effects may fall flat! For headings, <H ...> tags are the only safe bet.

Aligning text

HTML 3.0

Body text and headings are normally aligned to the left edge, but both can be set in the centre or to the right, if required.

To set the alignment, you write inside the <H ...> or <P> tag the keyword ALIGN = followed by *Center*, *Right* or *Left*. (Left is never needed – a simple <P> will left align text – but it can sometimes help to make the coding easier to read.)

For example:

```
<H2 ALIGN = "Right">
```

starts a right aligned heading. <H2> closes it.

```
<P ALIGN = "Center">
```

makes the following paragraph align to the centre of the window.

Note that the US spelling CENTER must be used in the tags.

This example demonstrates the ALIGN clause in action.

```
<HTML>
<H1 ALIGN = "Center"> Text Alignment</H1>
<P ALIGN = "Center">
Set in the centre of the window
<BR>
As many lines as you like from one ALIGN
<P>
Back to normal
<P ALIGN = "Right">
Align to the right
<P ALIGN = "Left">
Align to the left. This is the same as not setting an ALIGN
option. Note that long lines wrap round to fit the window size.
</HTML>
```

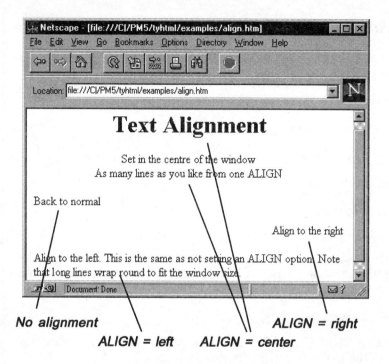

No alignment

ALIGN = left   **ALIGN = center**

ALIGN = right

<!COMMENTS>

Every HTML document has two aspects. There is the displayed page that the world will see, and the underlying source code, which is mainly of interest to you. If you want to add comments to the document, for your use and not for general consumption, write them inside <!...> tags, like this:

<! Written by me, with help from Harry>

<! Last modified 27/6/96>

<!...> is used in the next example.

Adding emphasis

If you want to emphasise a word or phrase in your text, you can use these pairs of tags.

<B> </B>

Sets text to **bold**.

<I> </I>

Makes text *italic*.

<TT> </TT>

This creates a 'typewriter' effect, by setting text in `Courier`.

These tags can be seen at work in the next example. This also demonstrates the use of an <!...> tag to write a hidden credit into the head of the document.

<STRONG> </STRONG>

<B>, <I> and <TT> are *physical* tags – they only work if the visitor's browser can display bold, italic or Courier fonts. <STRONG> is an example of a *logical* tag – one whose effect can be redefined at the receiving end. In practice, it will usually have the same emboldening effect as <B>. The subtle differences between logical and physical tags can be left to the experts.

<EM> </EM>

The EMPHASIS tag is the logical equivalent to <I>, and has the advantage of being more easily spotted when you are checking through your code for mistakes.

The other logical tags are **<CITE>**, **<CODE>** and **<KBD>**. They are all used in the same way as **<STRONG>**.

<BLINK> </BLINK>

Netscape Extension

This makes text flash – one way to catch people's attention!

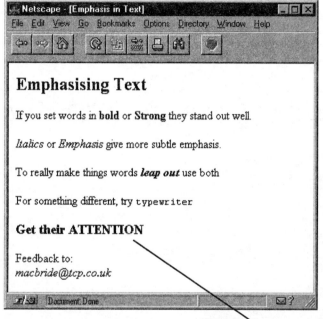

This flashes on and off

Different ways to catch people's eye. The code for this is overleaf.

SPACES IN CODE

Remember that the browser ignores surplus spaces. This means that you can happily put spaces around tags to make them more visible in your code, without creating nasty gaps on screen.

Compare the spacing in the code with the displayed result.

Try this HTML code to see the effect of the styling tags.

```
<HTML>
<HEAD>
</TITLE> Emphasis in Text </TITLE>
<! Written 19/3/96>                        Comment

</HEAD>                                    Spaces either side

<<H2> Emphasising Text </H2>

If you set words in  <B>  bold  </B> or  <STRONG>  Strong
</STRONG>  they stand out well.
<P>
<I> Italics </I> or <EM> Emphasis </EM> give more subtle
emphasis.
<P>
To really make things words <B> <I> leap out </I> </B> use both
<P>
For something different, try <TT> typewriter </TT>

<H3>Get their <BLINK> ATTENTION </BLINK> </H3>
<P>
Feedback to:
<ADDRESS>macbride@tcp.co.uk</ADDRESS>

</HTML>
```

SUPERSCRIPT and SUBSCRIPT

In HTML 3.0 you can also use the tags for
superscript and for subscript.

——— 2.7 Preformatted text ———

We noted earlier that when browsers are displaying HTML documents, they ignore all spaces and new lines. (They also ignore tabs!) Most of the time this is a good thing, as it means that you can spread out your document so that you can read it easily as source code, while using tags to create a displayed page which is also easy for your visitors to read. We have already covered the paragraph formatting tags, <P> and <BR>. There are more tags that can be used to create lists and tables, and we will come on to these later.

<PRE> </PRE>

These tags define preformatted text, and tell the browser to include the spaces, tabs and new lines, just as they are written. Within the <PRE> block, the text is displayed in Courier. This font does not use proportional spacing – i.e. every letter and space occupies the same width on screen. This means that you can use spaces to push text over to the right – and get it exactly where you want it. Tags are still obeyed, within the <PRE> block, so you can include headings, font sizes and alignments as usual.

Use <PRE> for price list, poems, or other text where the pattern of tabs and spaces is essential.

In this example, notice the pattern of indents and the right-aligned price list. Note also that the <H...> tags and ALIGN setting produce their usual effects.

Centred heading

```
<HTML>
<PRE>
<H3 ALIGN = "Center"> Rent-a-Rhyme </H3>
    There was a young netter called Seb
    Who put his Home page on the Web
        He said "What a drag
        I've missed out a tag
    The nerds will all think I'm a pleb"
```

2 levels of indents

```
<H4>Unbeatable prices!</H4>
    Limericks          4.99
    Clerihews          10.49
    Doggerel              25p per line
    Sonnets            39.99
    Free Verse         £POA
</PRE>
</HTML>
```

right-aligned prices

The <TABLE> facility (Chapter 8) lets you produce clear and attractive tables, but <PRE>formatting is a quick way to display colums of data.

QUOTES IN OPTIONS

Where you are setting an option, such as ALIGN = "Left", the quotes are not essential, but can be added for improved readability. You can also use any mix of lower case and capitals. ALIGN = LEFT, align = left, Align = "Left" all work.

──────────── 2.8 Colour ────────────

<Netscape Extension>

If you have been trying out the examples so far, you may have noticed that the text appears in black on a pale grey background, though some of the screenshots have a far better contrast between text and background. I confess, I have been changing the background colour and hiding the fact.

Now that we have got the main aspects of text formatting out of the way, and before we turn to graphics, let's spend a little time looking at how we can use colour.

<BODY BGCOLOR = *value*   TEXT = *value* >

You can set the colour of the background and of the text, by including either or both phrases in the <BODY ...> tag. These settings apply to the whole document.

<FONT COLOR = *value*>

This changes the colour of text, just as <FONT SIZE = ...> sets its size. Likewise, when you have done with a colour, you can switch to a new one with another <FONT COLOR = ... > tag, or restore the previous colour with </FONT>.

Colours are selected by giving the values, in hexadecimal, of the Red, Green and Blue components. If you understand RGB values and hex, then skip the next bit.

RGB colour

On a colour monitor (or TV), colours are produced by combining Red, Green and Blue light. Crudely, they combine like this:

	'Full Beam'	'Dipped'
Red + Green	Yellow	Brown
Red + Blue	Lilac	Magenta (Purple)
Green + Blue	Cyan	Turquoise
Red + Green + Blue	White	Grey

By varying the intensity of the three beams, you can produce the whole range of colours, and the intensity can be varied on a scale of 0 (off) to 255 (full beam). Except, you have to use hexadecimal. Time for digression number 2.

Hexadecimal

People naturally work in denary (base 10) because they have 10 fingers. Computers naturally work with binary (base 2) numbers,because they have two electronic 'fingers' – on and off. Binary numbers are dreadful for people to handle. (Read these two numbers aloud: 01001011 and 01011010. See what I mean?)

Hexadecimal (base 16) are a compromise choice. The numbers can be converted easily into binary (16 = 2 x 2 x 2 x 2) and can be read easily be people. The key point to note about hexadecimal is that it uses 16 'fingers', so the digits '0' to '9' are not enough. The letters 'A' to 'F' are pressed into service.

Base 10	Hex	
0	0	
...	...	
9	9	
10	A	
11	B	
12	C	
13	D	
14	E	
15	F	
16	10	(a 'handful')
32	20	
...etc		

Hexadecimal numbers are usually written as a pair of digits. To work out their base 10 value, multiply the first by 16 and add the second. For example:

2B	= 2 * 16 + 11(B)	= 43
80	= 8 * 16 + 0	= 128
FF	= 15(F) * 16 + 15	= 255

FF is the biggest number you can write with 2 digits. It is also the biggest value that can be held in 1 byte.

Colour values

Colours are set by giving what looks like a 6-digit hexadecimal number. It is actually 3 numbers, each of two digits, which set the brightness of the Red, Green and Blue components – in that order. On a 24-bit colour display, each of these could be a value between '00' and 'FF', but many of your visitors will be using a 256 or 16-colour display. In practical terms, it is enough to think of the light values as being '00' for *off*, '80' for *dipped* and 'FF' for *full beam*.

This table summarises the key colour values:

R	G	B	Colour
00	00	00	Black
FF	00	00	Bright Red
00	FF	00	Bright Green
00	00	FF	Bright Blue
80	00	00	Dark Red
00	80	00	Dark Green
00	00	80	Dark Blue
FF	FF	00	Bright Yellow
80	80	00	Brown
FF	00	FF	Magenta
80	00	80	Indigo
00	FF	FF	Bright Cyan
00	80	80	Turquoise
FF	FF	FF	White
80	80	80	Grey

To set the colours for the document, use the keywords 'BGCOLOR = ' and/or 'TEXT = ' with the appropriate values, inside the <BODY ....> tag. To set the colour for a section of text, use the keywords 'COLOR = ' inside a <FONT ...>.

By convention, the values are written in quotes with a preceding hash (#). These help to make the numbers stand out, but neither # nor quotes are necessary. Capital or lower case letters can be used for the hexadecimal digits A – F.

Examples:

```
<BODY BGCOLOR = "#80000">
```

sets the background to dark red.

```
<BODY TEXT = 0000FF>
```

sets the text colour to bright blue.

```
<BODY BGCOLOR = 000000 TEXT = FFFF00>
```

sets the background to black and the text to yellow.

```
<FONT COLOR = "#808080"> Donkey </FONT>
```

sets "Donkey" in grey, then reverts to the previous colour.

Use code like this to test out the range of colours:

```
<HTML>                                    set colours at the start
<BODY BGCOLOR = FFFFFF TEXT = 000000>
<H1>Colour test</H1>
<FONT SIZE = 5>                           COLOR – US spelling!
Let's get bright and cheerful
<BR><FONT COLOR = FF0000> Red             colour within
<BR><FONT COLOR = 00FF00> Green           the body text
<BR><FONT COLOR = 0000FF> Blue
<BR></FONT>Back to green, </FONT> then to red, </FONT>
then to black
</BODY>                  closing tag
</HTML>
```

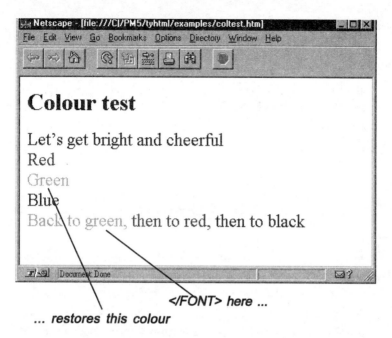

</FONT> here ...

... restores this colour

Sorry, couldn't persuade the publishers to do this page in colour, but you should be able to tell from the shades of grey that the colour does change. Notice how the </FONT> tags switch back to the previous colour, not to the one set by the TEXT option in the <BODY ...> tag.

2.9 Link colours

Netscape Extension

We will not be covering links until Chapter 4, but there is one aspect of them which is worth picking up now.

Links are normally displayed in blue, if they have not yet been used, or deep purple if they have. If you change the colour of your background, or of your text, the links may not stand out as well as you would like.

<BODY ... LINK = *value* **ALINK =** *value* **VLINK =** *value*>

Any or all of these options can be used to set the colour of the text that leads to:

> an unvisited link (LINK),
>
> the active link (ALINK),
>
> a visited link (VLINK).

The colour values are the same as for other settings.

—————— 2.10 Summary ——————

- There are simple, standard rules that apply to HTML tags.

- Most tags are used in pairs, with a </Closing tag> being used to mark the end of a formatted block.

- HTML documents can be written in Notepad or any word processor, but must be saved as plain text, with the .HTM extension to the filename.

- The <H...> tags provide a simple way to create headings. They set the size of text, embolden it and place it on a separate line.

- Use the <ADDRESS> pair of tags to add your e-mail address to the end of your document.

- Browsers normally ignore newlines, tabs and all excess spaces.

- Body text can be divided into paragraphs by the <P> tag, or placed on separate lines by inserting a <BR> break.

- You can control the size of words or single characters within the text using the SIZE = option in a <FONT> tag.

- You can add notes to your code by putting them in a <| ...> tag. Anything written in these will not be displayed.

- Body text and headings can be aligned to left, right or centre using the ALIGN = options.

- For emphasis, you can set your text in bold, italics or use a typewriter effect.

- Where you want to retain the spaces, tabs and newlines in your layout, use the <PRE> pair of tags to define it as preformatted text

- The colour of the background and text for the whole document can be set by options in the <BODY>tag.

- The colour of words and characters within the text can be set by the COLOR = option in a <FONT> tag.

- The colours used to identify link text can be set by the LINK, ALINK, VLINK options in the <BODY>tag.

3

GRAPHICS

Used thoughtfully, graphics can make a Web page a much more attractive and interesting place. By the time you reach the end of this chapter you should know how to create suitable graphics and how to place them where you want them on a page. On the way through we will have a look at two graphics packages that you may well find useful.

———— 3.2 Linking an image ————

<IMG SRC = "filename">

<IMG SRC ...> (IMaGe SouRCe) is the basic tag for linking an image into your page. Used without qualification, it places the image against the left edge, directly after any text, and with later text starting to its right.

For example:

```
<HTML>
<H2>Graphics</H2>
<IMG SRC = "ggnome.gif">
The Green Gnome
<P>My brother Gnoggin spends far too much time there!
</HTML>
```

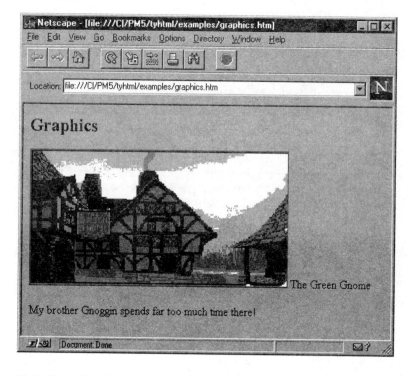

Note that following text will normally start at the lower right of the image. A <P> tag would push it onto the next line, or you could use an ALIGN qualifier – see below.

If the file is in the same directory as the HTML document, you only have to give its name – that was the case in the example above. If the image is stored elsewhere, you will have to include the path, to the directory.

In HTML, the path does not follow DOS rules. HTML was originally designed for Unix machines and it expects paths written the Unix way. Use forward slashes not backslashes, between directory names, and start with a forward slash. You also need to use a vertical bar line (|) and a slash, in place of the colon after the drive letter.

If you had a graphic MYPIC.GIF in a directory whose DOS path was C:\WINDOWS\TEMP, its HTML path would read:

/C|/WINDOWS/TEMP/MYPIC.GIF

That /forward slash at the start is essential.

TIP

Make life easy for yourself. While you are testing ideas, keep your graphics in the same directory as your HTML documents. When you put your page up on the Web, put all the files into one directory, (see Chapter 5).

——————— 3.3 Positioning ———————

ALIGN =

You have seen ALIGN used with the <P> and <H...> tags to align text to the left, right and centre. Used with images, it sets the vertical position in relation to surrounding text. There are three options: *Top*, *Middle* and *Bottom*. *Bottom* is the default, placing accompanying text at the bottom of the image.

If there is following text, and it is too long to fit in the remaining space to the right, it is wrapped round to below the image.

```
<HTML>
<H2>Graphics - Alignment</H2>
<FONT SIZE = 4>
Text before
<IMG SRC = "arrows.gif" ALIGN = Middle>
Text after. Long sentences wrap round to below the image
</FONT>
</HTML>
```

Quotes are optional but make names stand out

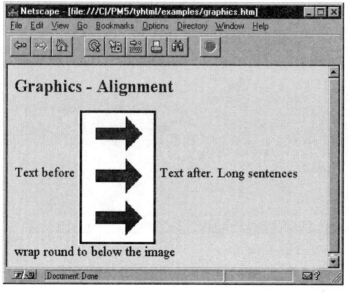

If you want to title your image, a <H...> tag will push the heading onto a new line. Use FONT SIZE to place enlarged text beside the image. Where text is so long that it will wrap round below the image, use ALIGN = Bottom. ALIGN = Middle looks a mess, as you can see, ALIGN = Top is even worse! Alternatively, use a Table to set a block of text alongside an image – see Chapter 8.

\<CENTER\>

Netscape Extension

When looking at text alignment in the last chapter, we met the ALIGN = "Center" option for paragraphs and headings. \<CENTER\> can also be used as a tag in its own right to align text *and graphics* in the centre of the display window. When used in this way, a closing \</CENTER\> tag is needed at the end of the centred material. For example:

```
<HTML>
<H3>Positioning Graphics</H3>
<CENTER><IMG SRC = "smiley.gif"></CENTER>
</HTML>
```

CENTE̲R – US spelling

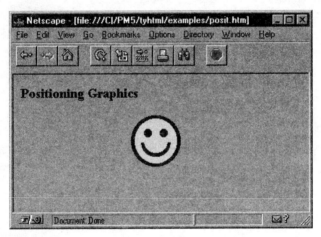

If this had been written:

```
<HTML>
<CENTER>
<H3>Positioning Graphics</H3>
<IMG SRC = "smiley.gif"></CENTER>
</HTML>
```

both the heading and image would have been centred.

Spacing

There are two options that can control the spacing around graphics. The default settings are to leave a space of 10 pixels above and below an image, and about 6 pixels to either side.

HSPACE = sets the pixel spacing to the left and right;
VSPACE = sets the pixel spaces above and below the image.

Note that you cannot control left and right, or above and below spacing independently.

Unless you are aiming for a particularly 'spaced-out' look, the HSPACE and VSPACE values should not be too large. In the example below they have been exaggerated so that their effects are clearly visible. compare these with the first two graphics, which are placed at the default spacing.

```
<HTML>
<TITLE>Graphics Spacing</TITLE>
<BODY BGCOLOR = 80FF80 TEXT = 00008F>
<IMG SRC = "arrow1.gif" ALIGN = Middle> Buy now! <P>
<IMG SRC = "arrow1.gif" ALIGN = Middle> Huge savings!<P>
<IMG SRC = "arrow1.gif" ALIGN = Middle VSPACE = 25>
Unrepeatable bargains!! <P>
<IMG SRC = "arrow1.gif" ALIGN = Middle HSPACE = 50>
Don't miss it!!!!
</BODY>
</HTML>
```

BORDERS

You can put a border around an image by including the option BORDER = ... setting the thickness in pixels. e.g.

```
<IMG SRC = "mypic.gif" ALIGN = Middle BORDER = 5>
```

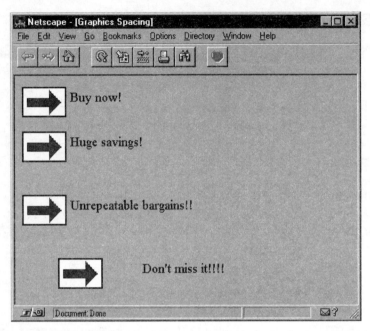

Spacing around graphics makes them stand out, but don't overdo it!

3.4 Adjusting the size

$\langle$ *Netscape Extension* $\rangle$

Normally you would want your graphics to be displayed at their natural size, but there are some times when it is useful to be able to adjust the size of the displayed image. There is little point in showing an image at a reduced size – you may as well make it smaller to start with, and save the reduced image to file. If you make the display larger than the original, it keeps down the size of the graphics file and the download time, though it will produce a lower resolution, chunkier image. This won't matter if the original picture was simple and chunky anyway, but would not be advisable for photographs or scanned art.

HTML gives us two alternative ways of setting the size:

● fixed, where the displayed size is given in pixels – it helps if you know the size of the original;
● variable, where the size is specified as a percentage of the screen size.

The advantage of the variable approach is that you can be sure that your image will fit on screen, whatever the size of your visitors' windows. We'll come back to that in our second example.

HEIGHT = *value* WIDTH = *value*

The same tag options are used for fixed and variable resizing. The only difference is in how you give the values.

For **fixed** sizing, simply give the pixels as plain numbers:

HEIGHT = 100 WIDTH = 75

Sets the displayed size of the image at 100 x 75 pixels. If you want to avoid distorting the shape, you must know the original pixel size, so that you can calculate the new values.

For **variable** sizing, give the value as a percentage of the screen height or width, and follow the number with a % sign.

HEIGHT = 50%

Sets the image to be scaled down so that it fills half the height of the browser window.

WIDTH = 25%

Scales the image down to fit into a quarter of the width of the window.

If you only set one value, the same scaling is applied in both directions. Set HEIGHT *and* WIDTH only if it is essential that the image occupies a certain amount of space in both directions – you can guarantee that few of your visitors will be using the same shape of browser window as you, so that most will get a distorted image.

```
<HTML>
<TITLE>Graphics Sizing</TITLE>
<BODY BGCOLOR = FFFFFF>
<IMG SRC = "compass.gif"> Original size 60 x 60
<IMG SRC = "compass.gif" HEIGHT = 90 WIDTH = 90>
Increased to 90 x 90 <BR>
<IMG SRC = "compass.gif" HEIGHT = 50%> Sized to fill half
of the screen height <BR>
<IMG SRC = "compass.gif" WIDTH = 10%> Sized to fill a
tenth of the width
</BODY>
</HTML>
```

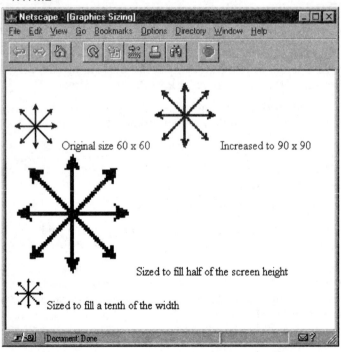

Enlarged images rarely look as good as the originals.

If you want to start your page with a bang, you can use a graphic instead of a <H ...> heading. Even if you only use text, at least you can have coloured text and set in any font that your computer can produce. With a normal <H ...> heading, it will be wrapped round if your visitor is working in a narrow window. With a graphic as a heading, there is a danger that half of it will disappear off the edge of a visitor's window. And this is where percentage resizing really comes into its own. In the example below, the title will always occupy 80% of the width of the window – whatever its width.

With percentage scaling, you will always get a perfect fit for your graphics.

```
<HTML>
<BODY BGCOLOR = FFFFFF>
<CENTER>
<IMG SRC = "grafhead.gif" WIDTH = 80%>
<H2>Web Weavers Hand-knitted T-shirts</H2>
</CENTER>
<P>
```

For that perfect fit in T-shirts, order yours now from Web Weavers.

```
<P>
<BODY>
</HTML>
```

——— 3.5 Background images ———

Netscape Extension

Another striking use for an image is as a background to your page. The trick here is *not* to use a large, full-page picture – which will take an age to download – but to use a small image. HTML automatically repeats any image used as a background, so you can get a full screen from the tiniest images.

With any kind of background pattern, it is important that the pattern does not become too dominant – it is supposed to be a background after all. The answer is either to use a very sparse pattern, or pale colours. You can see examples of both here.

This first page has a 'deep space' background, formed by repeating this scatter of stars. The original image is about 200 pixels square, and as a GIF file, takes less than 500 bytes. Used with bright yellow or cyan text, it is striking, but still produces a readable page.

```
<HTML>
<HEAD>
<TITLE>
BACKGROUND GRAPHICS
</TITLE>
</HEAD>
<BODY>
<BODY BACKGROUND = "stars.gif" TEXT = FFFF00>
<FONT SIZE = 7>
One for the Star Trek fans
<FONT SIZE = 5>
<P>
The simpler the background, the better
</BODY>
</HTML>
```

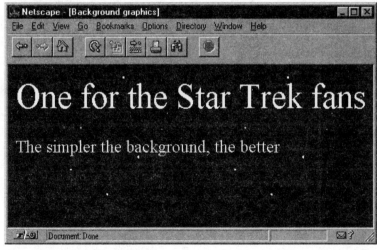

The second example uses a proper pattern. This one is based on the TRIANGLES.BMP, one of the 'wallpapers' supplied with Windows 95. The original image is minute – but it tiles to good effect. It also has strong contrasts, which is not so good. Whether you use dark or light text, parts of it will be unreadable against some areas of the pattern.

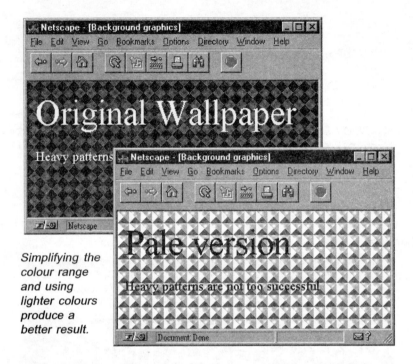

Simplifying the colour range and using lighter colours produce a better result.

Look out for background images as you surf the Web. You can see the star pattern and others at the Teach Yourself test site:

www.tcp.co.uk/~macbride

3.6 File formats

Web standards

You may have noticed that in the examples so far, I have used GIF files. GIF (Graphic Information Format) was established by CompuServe as the standard for graphics used in their communication services. It was chosen because its built-in compression produces very compact files. For this same reason it has been adopted as a standard for Web browsers.

The second widely-used standard format is JPEG (Joint Photographic Experts Group) – on PCs the files have a JGP extension. This also produces compact files. If you are storing a 256-colour image, it will generally, but not always, be smaller as a GIF – JPGs seem to handle more complex images more compactly that GIFs. If you want to store a 24-bit colour image, such as a Kodak PhotoCD snapshot, you must use JPG, as GIFs can only cope with 256 colours.

Both GIF and JPG formats can be handled by the internal viewers of Web browsers. Your visitors will only be able to see graphics in other formats if they have configured suitable external viewers.

Other formats

Someone once commented that the computing industry must love standards as they have so many of them! This is certainly true with graphic 'standard' formats. There are dozens of them. On a Windows system, without any other software, you can produce graphics in 3 different BMP formats, and as CLP (Clipboard) files – and probably also as PCX files. Add in a decent word-processor and you can produce WMF (Windows Meta File) graphics (Microsoft Word) or WPG files (WordPerfect). And this is before you start on the drawing and painting programs, or importing images through a scanner (BMP, PCX or TIFF) or from Kodak PhotoCD (PCD).

The simple fact is that you can probably produce graphics in half a dozen or more formats from your existing software, but GIF and JPG will not be amongst them! If you want to include pictures in your pages, you will need graphics software that can convert your files into GIFs or JPGs.

3.7 Graphics software

There are a number of freeware, shareware and commercial programs around that will convert graphics. Let's have a look at two of the best. Both of these can do more than just conversion. You can also use them to scale, crop, recolour, rotate, mirror, filter, edit and otherwise manipulate your images before you put them on display.

Lview Pro

Lview Pro is a neat and efficient piece of software. It can convert graphics in the more common formats into either GIFs or JPG files; it has a good set of editing tools; and it has two big advantages over alternative graphics software – it is free (for

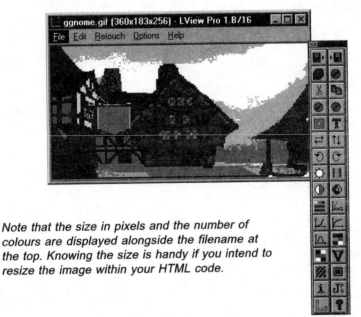

Note that the size in pixels and the number of colours are displayed alongside the filename at the top. Knowing the size is handy if you intend to resize the image within your HTML code.

personal use only), and the package is relatively compact, so it takes only a megabyte or so on the disk and loads up quickly.

When you open a file in Lview Pro, the window adapts to the size of the graphic, and the toolbar is placed on or beside the picture, for easy access.

You may well find the tool icons somewhat cryptic. However, if you place the cursor over a tool a 'tooltip' will pop up to tell you its name. You can also access the same comands through the menus. Some of the names and menu items may also not mean

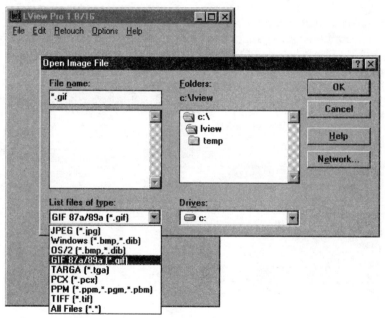

You can see the types of files that can be handled by Lview Pro in this screenshot of the Open File dialog box. These include GIF and JPG (which you will need for your Web pages) and the BMP and PCX formats that are commonly produced by Windows programs.

If the formats that you are likely to use are all in the list, then this is the graphics software to go for.

a lot to you, but at least you have got something you can look up in the Help pages. These are brief, but generally adequate, and most of the operations are straightforward.

Resizing

This is one of the easiest, but most useful, operations. Large images can often be reduced down to half size (and about a quarter of their file size), without significant loss of detail.

The command **Edit | Resize** opens the **Resize Image** dialog box. This shows the current size, and a range of options for changing it. If you need your picture to be a very specific size, you can type the new values in, but usually the simplest approach is to click on one or other of the sliders – they both move together – to set a new ratio.

Images lose very little detail when reduced to 75% of their original size.

Enlarging images is rarely as successful. Details become granular, and smooth curves turn into stepped lines. If you really must enlarge, then you could try using the **Retouch | Image Filters ...** options to smooth the edges again.

Transparent backgrounds

With Lview Pro, you can set the background of your image to be transparent when viewed on your page. This is irrelevant for photographs or other full pictures, but is very useful for the blobs that you might use for bullets (see Chapter 6). Of course, you can colour your original image so that it has the same background colour as your page, but that implies that (a) you have already fixed on your page colour, and (b) you will only use the image on that one page or others of the same colour.

If you want to give an image a transparent background, it will be simplest if the background of the original image is an easily identifiable colour. Make it black or white when you are creating the image.

When you take it into Lview Pro, select the **Options | Background colour** command. A palette opens, showing the full range of colours used in the image.

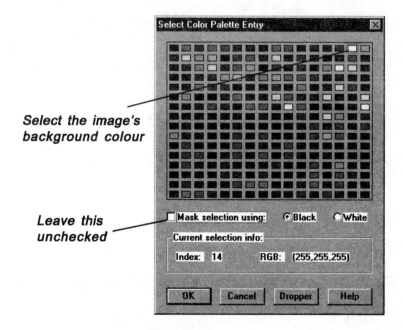

Select the image's background colour

Leave this unchecked

Click on the image's background colour, leave the **Mask selection using:** box unchecked and click OK. Save the graphic as a GIF or JPG as usual. That should be all there is to it.

The image can now be incorporated into your pages in the usual way. In this screenshot, you can see three versions of the same image. The top one is in its original state; the second had white selected as background; the bottom one had red selected – that was obviously a mistake!

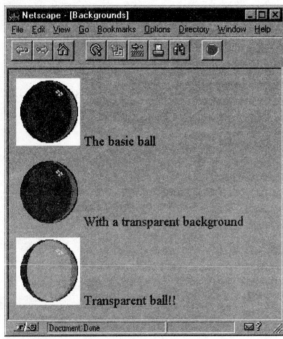

You can make the background show through any part of the image – it all depends upon the colour that you select. Experiment with the effects.

Your service provider may have a copy of LviewPro, but if not, it is readily available on the Internet. Amongst other places you can get it from Washington State's software archive:

ftp://Wuarchive.wustl.edu/systems/ibmpc/win3/desktop/lviewp1b.zip

PaintShop Pro

PaintShop Pro is a well-specified and full-featured professional tool. It is shareware, offered with a free 30-day trial for evaluation and a purchase price (at the time of writing) of £50. It is produced by Jasc Inc., and can be downloaded from their Web site at:

> http://www.jasc.com

File formats

PaintShop Pro can handle far more graphics formats than Lview Pro: BMP, CDR, CGM, CLP, DIB, GEM, GIF, HGL, JASC, JIF, JPG, PCD, PCX, PGM, PIC, PSD, RLE, TGA, TIFF, WPG, WMF – many in several different versions. And that list only includes the main ones! If you have got an application that can produce a drawn or painted image, it is a fair bet that PaintShop Pro can read it. And if it can read the file, it can convert it into a GIF or JPG for inclusion in your page.

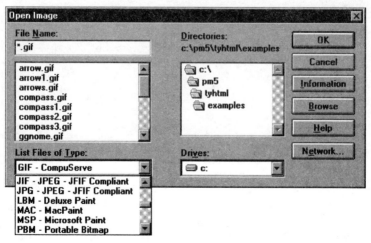

*You can see part of the **List Files of Type:** list in the illustration. It should be enough to give you an inkling of the conversion power of this software.*

If you have a whole set of files that you want to include in your pages – you might be a keen photographer or artist and be aiming to put on an exhibition, then PaintShop Pro's batch conversion facility will be appreciated.

In batch conversion, you simply select a set of files of one type to be opened and specify the output type. It then processes the lot, retaining the filenames but replacing the extension.

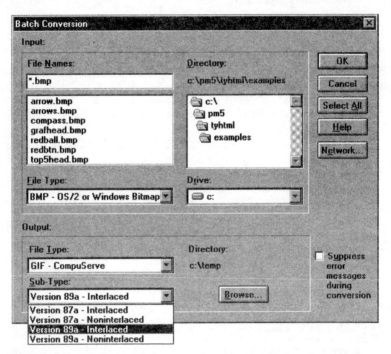

When setting the output type, you often have a choice of versions. With GIFs, go for one or other of the 89a versions.

Other features

Though PaintShop Pro offers little more than LviewPro in terms of image manipulation and editing, it does it in a much more user-friendly way, backed up by a very extensive Help system.

For example, when applying a filter to smooth, blur, sharpen or whatever, it gives you a preview of the effect before you commit yourself to it.

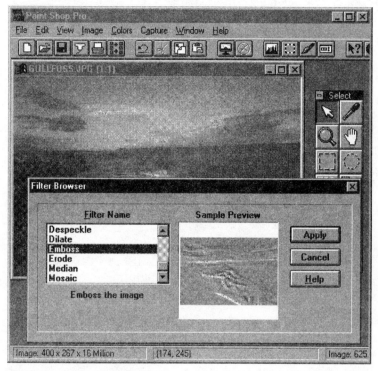

The Sample Preview provides a quick way of checking whether or not an effect will work.

PaintShop Pro also allows you to have any number of pictures open at a time, so that you can have 'before' and 'after' copies of the same image – and scrap the 'after' if your editing didn't work!

Transparent GIFs can be produced, if required, by setting the Options in the Save As routine.

3.8 Summary

● Images can be placed in a page with the <IMG SRC = ...> tag.

● The ALIGN = option can be used to align following text with the top, middle or bottom of an image.

● Images can be centred on a page with <CENTER>.

● The size of an image can be fixed, or made relative to the browser window size, using the WIDTH = and HEIGHT = options.

● The <BODY BACKGROUND = ...> option allows you to fill the background of the page with a single image, or a repeated pattern of a small image.

● All browsers can display graphics in GIF or JPG formats. Other formats create problems.

● To convert graphics into different formats, you need software such as LView Pro and PaintShop Pro. These packages can also be used for manipulating images in many ways.

4

LINKS

4.1 Aims of this chapter

Graphics are fun, formatted text reads well, but when it comes to the crunch, hypertext links are what HTML is all about. In this chapter you will see how to create interlocking links between your home page and other pages of your own, links to other people's pages elsewhere on the Web, links within a page so that readers can jump from one part to another, and links to multimedia and other files.

4.2 HREF

The key word for links is HREF (Hypertext REFerence). This identifies the target page, or point within a page. But it can't be used by itself. It must be anchored to a piece of text or a graphic, so that there is something to click on to pick up the link. The *anchor* tags are <A ...> and </A> which mark the start and end of the link text.

The two are used together to create the link and its jumping off point. For example:

<A HREF = "http://www.yahoo.com"> Go to Yahoo </A>

Let's break that down:

<A HREF =	marks the start of the tag.
http://	identifies it a World Wide Web link. You could miss this out and the link would still work – browsers assume that a link is to a Web page unless they are told differently. But if you do want another type of link, you must include its identifier (see section 4.7).
www.yahoo.com	the URL of the target – this is the home page of the great Yahoo directory.
Go to Yahoo	is the link text that will be underlined when viewed in a browser, and can be clicked to make the connection.
</A>	marks the end of the link text.

You can use different types of links, and replace the text by an image, but all hypertext links follow this pattern.

URLs

Every page, file, directory, site and person on the Internet has its own URL – Uniform Resource Locator. The basic pattern is always the same:

type://HostComputerAddress/Directory/Filename

Type	Identifies
http://	Web page
file://	file in a local directory
ftp://	file that can be downloaded via FTP
news://	link to a newsgroup
mailto://	e-mail address of a person

———— 4.3 Links to other pages ————

These are the simplest to handle, especially where the link is to the home page of a well-established site. Just use the http:// identifier (or miss it out) and give the address as in the example opposite.

Here are some more examples – and they are to places that you should have in your own Bookmark file:

<A HREF = "http://www.lycos.com"> Lycos </A>

<A HREF = "http://www.mckinley.com"> Magellan </A>

<A HREF = "http://www.ukdirectory.com"> UK Directory </A>

<A HREF = "http://www.shareware.com"> c|net Shareware </A>

Lycos and Magellan are both excellent places to start searching for information, files or other resources. The UK Directory is one of the best sites for picking up links to UK business, schools, colleges and individuals' home pages. c|net run one of America's brightest news, reviews and resources sites.

If you are linking to a page or file in a sub-directory, or to the home page of another user, then there are two points that need special attention.

● You must get the page address absolutely right – using upper and lower case and punctuation exactly according to the URL.

● You must check the link regularly to make sure that it is still there. People have a nasty habit of reorganising their directories, or moving from one service to another, just after you have included the link in your page!

Exact addresses

The first step in setting up any link is to get the exact address. The best way to do that is to go there yourself – which guarantees that you have the address right – then copy the address from the Location slot at the top of the browser.

If you highlight it and use **Edit|Copy**, rather than copying it by hand, you can be sure of not making a mistake. The address can then be pasted into your HTML document.

Edit|Copy *the address and* **Paste** *it into your document*

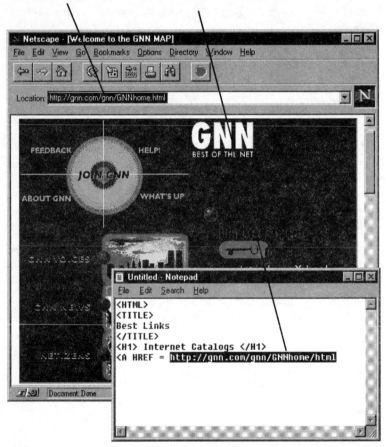

The Copy and Paste approach avoids all errors, but is not always convenient – you may not want to start editing an HTML document half way through a surfing session. Just make sure you write down addresses exactly as you see them.

In particular, watch out for:

● the use of underlines and capital letters

  http://www.yahoo.com/Computers_and_Internet

  this is the Computers and Internet menu at Yahoo.

● tildes (~), used to indicate an individual user's page

  http://www.tcp.co.uk/~macbride/tybooks.html

  my 'Teach Yourself books' page at Total Connectivity Providers.

● version numbers, dates and similar things that are likely to change

  http://www.access.digex.net/~ikind/babel96a.html

  this is BABEL, a glossary of abbreviations and acronyms, in its first 1996 update. This site will need revisiting regularly to check the URL.

Your other pages

OK! I know you haven't got your first home page up yet, unless you have skipped ahead, but let's do this while we are on links.

If you do not have a lot to say, a single page will do the job, but it is a different matter if you want to publish a lot of information, or cover several distinct areas – you, your job, your hobby and your holiday snaps; your firm's four product lines; the two clubs that you run; separate home pages for you, your partner, your kids, your granny and your cat ... or whatever. These could all result in long, slow-to-download pages. A better solution is to have several pages, all accessible from the top one. Your visitors can then go quickly to the page that interests them.

The pages should all be stored in the same directory – now, on your system while you are testing them, and later when you upload them to your service provider. The link is then a very simple one, consisting only of the filename:

```
<A HREF = "tiddles.htm"> My Cat's Home Page </A>
```

The linked pages, in a multi-page set should all have a link back to the top level home page. Here's a skeleton set:

The top level. Filename = *index.html*

```
<HTML>
<TITLE> My Home Page </TITLE>
<BODY>
...
<A HREF = "myjob.htm"> My Job </A>
<A HREF = "myhobby.htm"> My Hobby </A>
<A HREF = "links.htm"> Favourite Places </A>
<A HREF = "author.htm"> All about me </A>
...
</BODY>
</HTML>
```

Linked page. Filename = *myjob.htm*

```
<HTML>
<TITLE> My Job </TITLE>
<BODY>
I work for .......
<A HREF = "index.html"> Return to the top </A>
</BODY>
</HTML>
```

COME UP AND SEE ME SOMETIME

For a more fully worked example of a multi-page set, drop in on my home page:

www.tcp.co.uk/~macbride

———4.4 Links within documents———

If you want to jump from one part of a document to another –
perhaps from a menu at the top, down to a section, or back up to
the top – you have to define the points to jump to. These are
marked by a variation on the anchor tag:

<A NAME = *jumppoint*> jump point text </A>

The jump point can be a single word or phrase, and you can
write it in quotes if you want to make it stand out more clearly
in the source code. It will not be identified in the display – there
is no reason to do so, as this is a place that you arrive at, not
somewhere to go from. The <A NAME = ...> tag can therefore be
wrapped around an existing heading, or embedded in body text
at the right place.

These are both acceptable uses:

<A NAME = my job> I work </A> for .....

<A NAME = "backup"> Welcome </A>

At the jumping-off point, use an HREF tag, as with other links:

<A HREF = #*jumppoint*> text </A>

Notice the hash (#) before the *jumppoint* name. It is crucial. If
you miss it out, the browser will think that you are trying to
make a simple link to another page in your directory.

As with other links, it is vital to use exactly the same punctuation
and upper/lower case characters in the HREF as in the NAME.

<A HREF = #Me> All About Me </A>

will not find:

<A NAME = me> I am </A> nearly 9 and have surfed for...

because "me" and "Me" are two different things.

In the example below, the home page will have four sections,
when it is finished. At this stage, the first two are in place and
can be jumped to from the Contents list at the top.

Notice that both have jumps at the end to take the visitor back up to the top of the page.

```
<HTML>
<TITLE>Jumps</TITLE>
<BODY BGCOLOR = FFFFFF TEXT = 000000>
```
"top" jump point
```
<H1> <A NAME = "top"> Welcome </A> </H1>
```
Jump to "me"
```
<HR>
<H2>Contents </H2>
<H3><A HREF = "#me"> This is Me </A>
```
Jump to "my job"
```
<BR><A HREF = "#my job"> My Job </A>
<BR>The Cleethorpes Surfing Club
<BR>My Cat's home page
```
"me" jump point
```
<HR>
<H2> <A NAME = "me"> All about me </A> </H2>
What a fascinating chap I am...(more lies...)
<P>
```
Jump back to "top"
```
<A HREF = "#top"> Return to the top </A>
```
"my job" jump point
```
<HR>
<A NAME = "my job"> <H2> My Job </H2> </A>
I'm a Careers Adviser, and let me give you some advice -
don't choose this as a career. <P>
<A HREF = "#top"> Return to the top </A>
</BODY>
```
Jump back to "top"
```
</HTML>
```

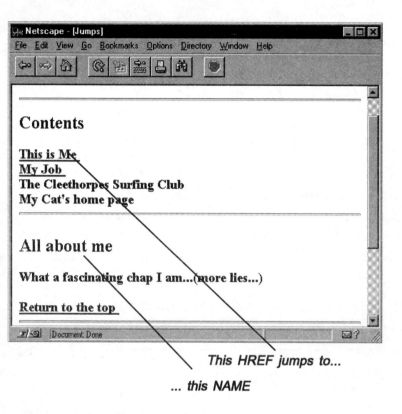

This HREF jumps to...

... this NAME

Reaching other directories

Keeping everything in the same directory is always the simplest solution, but if you have to reference pages, graphics or any other files in other directories, here are the rules.

If the file is in a sub-directory of the one holding the page that calls for it, use the pattern *directory_name / filename*:

    <A HREF = "holiday/snapbook.htm">

finds the *snapbook.htm* page in the *holiday* sub-directory.

To get back up from a sub-directory, use double dots (..). e.g.

    <A HREF = "../index.htm">

will take you back to the index page in the directory above.

If you need to refer to a file somewhere else on the system – not in the path above or below where the HREF is located – you will have to give the full path, from the root, down to the directory. Remember – the path starts with a forward slash, to specify the current system, and you must use a vertical bar line (|) and a slash, in place of the colon after the drive letter. For example:

    <A HREF = "/C|/graphics/gallery.htm">

When you upload your files to your service provider, check first with them to find the correct path to your place in their system.

TIP

You can add *file://* before the link to define its type, but it works just as well – and sometimes better – without!

Jump points on other pages

If you want to be very precise in your linking to other pages, you can set up a link to a NAMEd jump point in another page.

    <A HREF = "cats.htm#tiddles"> Go to Tiddles corner </A>

This will link to the *cats.htm* page, jumping to the *tiddles* part of it.

Jump point references can be added to links to other pages elsewhere on the Web, as long as you know the NAME. This will jump-link to the updated links section of my *Teach Yourself HTML* page:

<A HREF = "www.tcp.co.uk/~macbride/tybooks#links">

....assuming that I haven't changed the page by then.

———— 4.5 Links and images ————

Linking tags do not have to be attached to text. You can anchor them to graphics, replacing the text with an <IMG SRC = ...> tag.

For example:

    <A HREF = www.netscape.com> <IMG SRC = logo.gif> </A>

That would create a link to Netscape's home page, based on the image of their logo. Look for the image link in this next example.

    <HTML>
    <TITLE>Meggieland</TITLE>
    <H2>Welcome to Cleethorpes</H2>
    <A HREF = meggies.html> <IMG SRC = meggies.gif></A>

On screen, an image holding a link is outlined, in the same way that text with a link is underlined – unless you have changed the defaults.

```
<P><A HREF = surfsup.htm> Surfing the North Sea </A>
<P><A HREF = tweet.htm> The Budgie-Fancier's Paradise </A>
</HTML>
```

An image certainly has more impact than text, but if your visitors choose not to download images, they will have nothing to see. The solution lies in the ALT option. This defines text to be displayed if images are not downloaded. The option is unusual in that you must put quotes around your text if you have more than one word. Miss them out, and only the first word will be displayed. If we edit the text to read:

```
<A HREF = meggies.html> <IMG SRC = meggies.gif ALT =
"How to get there"></A>
```

Then a text-only visitor will see this.

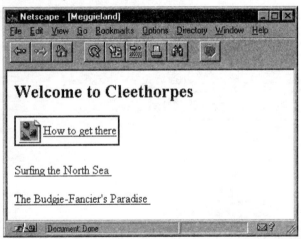

TIP

Attach an ALT option to any graphic, so that your visitors can tell what they will get before they download it.

```
<IMG SRC = beauty.gif ALT = "Picture of me, 389Kb">
```

At least they have been warned.

4.6 Multimedia links

Think twice – then think again – before including a multimedia clip in your home page. With video clips, you only get around 5 or 6 seconds of playing time in 1 megabyte, and that will take up to 20 minutes to download; audio clips are more compact at around 5 seconds per 100Kb (2 minutes downloading). Any multimedia clip that you put on your page must be worth viewing – do you really expect your visitors to wait 5 minutes to hear you give a short greeting? If you are in the video or music business and you want to offer demos, that is another matter, as people will – you hope – be visiting your site to get the demos.

There is also a practical problem to face. Does your service provider allow you enough Web storage space for the files? Some of the less generous providers restrict their users to as little as 100Kb of space; even CompuServe's 1Mb allowance will not go far if you are into multimedia.

If, after all, you do want to include multimedia clips, remember that your visitors will only be able to view them if they have the right software. AVI and WAV files should present few problems for most visitors, as these can be handled by the standard Windows Media Player. If you are using other types, then it might be an idea if you also included a link to an FTP site where your visitors could find the necessary viewing software.

Multimedia files are pulled into a page with the HREF link.

```
<A HREF = "newwave.avi">
New video from the hottest rock group in Neasden (959Kb)
</A>

<A HREF = "hello.wav"> Hello from me (257Kb) </A>
```

Do include the file size in the accompanying text.

For the following example, I have used a promotional clip from *Toystory* – mainly because it is such a marvellous movie, and I had the clip lying around. However, this example is not going up on my home page. You cannot publish anyone else's videos or other work without their permission! You should assume that everything that you see on the Internet is the copyright of the person who put it there – always check before you re-use anything on your own published pages.

```
<HTML>
<TITLE> Multimedia Links </TITLE>
<BODY BGCOLOR = FFFFFF TEXT = 000000>
<H2>The best computer animation to date </H2>
<A HREF = storybit.avi> <IMG SRC = toystory.gif BORDER =2>
<P> Clip from Toystory demo 2.3 Mb </A>
</BODY>
</HTML>
```

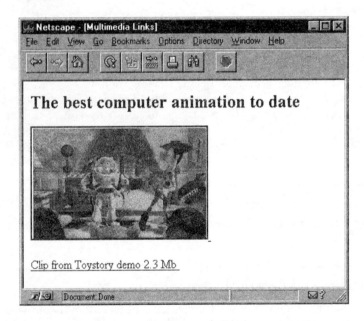

If you are linking to a video (your own, remember), then include a still on your page to give your visitors a taste of what's to come.

4.7 Links off the Web

HTML links are not restricted to local files and pages on the World Wide Web. You can also create links to other parts of the Internet. Three types of links are particularly worth noting.

FTP

FTP is the Internet's standard File Transfer Protocol. It defines the way that files are transferred over the Internet. FTP sites are host computers with (some) directories open to the public, and suitable software to enable users to download files from – and upload them to – their directories. Web browsers have limited FTP capabilities built into them, so that they can download from FTP sites. If you want to upload, you need WS_FTP (see the next chapter). If you want to run an FTP site, you need another book!

You may have uploaded files, such as programs that you have written, pictures that you have created or whatever, to an FTP site, or found good software on an FTP site. If you want the world to know about them, and to be able to access them from your home page, you need a link like this:

```
<A HREF = ftp://kth.se/pub/tex/tools/pkzip/pkz204g.exe>
Download PKZIP (197Kb) </A>
```

Notice that the link starts with ftp://, so the browser knows how to handle it, and includes the site name and full path down to the file. The text should make it clear that the link will download a file, and – if possible – should give the file size.

If you just want to point people towards a good site, you can still use ftp://, but link to a site address, or a directory within it. The browser will display a directory listing when the link is used.

```
<A HREF = ftp://micros.hensa.ac.uk/mirrors/cica/> The UK
mirror of the great CICA site </A>
```

UPDATING LINKS

If you include links to files and directories at FTP sites, be prepared to revisit regularly to check that they are still there, and still in the same place. Nothing stays the same for long on the Internet!

Newsgroups

With something like 10,000 newsgroups now circulated over the Internet, and no single controlling organisation, finding those devoted to any given interest can take time. For instance, there are music newsgroups in the alt, bit, claru, fido and rec heirarchies, plus a couple of dozen in other small news sets – over a hundred groups in total, covering every possible musical taste. If you have taken the trouble to track down and try them out, and can recommend a few that carry good, relevant articles about one particular field of music, why not offer your visitors links to selected groups. The link will take the form:

    <A HREF = news://alt.music.pink.floyd> THE GROUP! </A>

... or whatever your taste may be.

E-mail

Last, but by no means least, is *mailto:*. This gives a simple means for your visitors to contact you by e-mail. It will call up the mail creation window, with your address in the Mail To: slot, and will send the mail directly once it has been written.

    <A HREF = mailto:jobloggs@yournet.co.uk> Mail me! </A>

Note: *Do not start the URL with* // *if your mailbox is on the same server as your Web page.*

Here are the new link types in use in a page:

```
<HTML>
<TITLE>Links Off the Web</TITLE>
<BODY BGCOLOR = FFFFFF>
<H3>Links elsewhere in the Internet</H3>
<A HREF = ftp://kth.se/pub/tex/tools/pkzip/pkz204g.exe>
Download PKZIP (197Kb) </A>
<P>
<A HREF = ftp://micros.hensa.ac.uk/mirrors/cica/>The UK
mirror of the great CICA archives </A>
<P>
<A HREF = news://rec.humour.funny> <IMG SRC = smiley.gif
ALT = "rec.humour.funny"> Have a laugh </A>
<P>
Feedback:<A HREF = mailto:macbride@tcp.co.uk>Mail to
Mac </A>
<P>
</BODY>
</HTML>
```

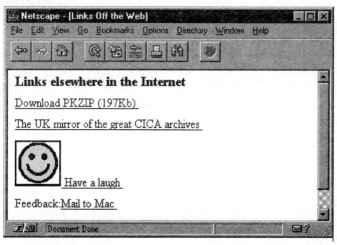

─────── 4.8 Summary ───────

- The <A HREF = ...> tag set up a hypertext link to another page or file within your system or elsewhere on the Internet.

- When linking to other pages, use the http:// prefix. Always double-check the address after you have typed it – they are easy to get wrong!

- Using <A NAME = ...> you can mark a point within a document, that can be jumped to. The incoming jump can originate within the same document, or from elsewhere on the Web.

- The start point for a hypertext link can be an item of text or an image – or both.

- When using an image as a link, you should include ALT text for visitors who do not download the graphics automatically.

- Links to multimedia files use the same <A HREF = ...> tag.

- If you want to include multimedia files in your pages, do check that your service provider will allow you enough storage space for them.

- If you have a set of linked pages, or are using images and other files in your pages, you will save yourself trouble if you keep all your files in the same directory.

- Using *ftp://*, *news://* and other prefixes, you can link to Internet resources outside the Web.

- The *mailto:* link allows visitors to send e-mail to you easily.

5

ONTO THE WEB

——— 5.1 Aims of this chapter ———

So, you are ready to offer your efforts to the world! And why
not? In this chapter we will work through the stages of publishing
your pages on the Web. We will look at what you need to do
beforehand, uploading your pages and testing the results. When
you have a site worth seeing, then you will want to let people
know about it, and that is covered in the final part of this chapter.

——— 5.2 Getting ready ———

Your Files

When your page(s) and images are uploaded to your service
provider's computer, they will normally all be stored in one
directory. (You may be able to create sub-directories within your
part of their system, but that creates complexities you do not
need.) Set up a new directory on your own system and copy into

it the HTML documents and graphics files that make up your home page set. Having everything you need in one place – a place that is not cluttered up with unwanted files – will make life easier when you upload.

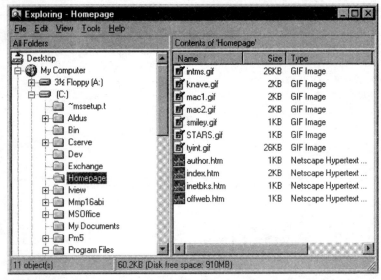

Get all the documents and graphic files together in a special directory.

Final test

Run your browser, turn off the image loading and open your home page file. How does it look as a text-only page? If you have several linked pages, use the links to check out each one. Can you move between all the pages? Do they all look OK in text-only mode?

Work through the pages again, downloading the images as you go. Are all the images displayed correctly? Are you happy with the layout? If you have any design changes to make, now is the time to do it. (Though you can edit and upload new versions of your pages – or add more, delete or replace the lot – at any point in the future.)

Your Service Provider

Before you can upload to your service provider, you need to know where to put your files, how to get them there, and what to call your home page – the top one of the set – when it is on site.

At CompuServe, all home pages are called *homepage.htm*; at TCP, another provider that I use, the home page must be called *index.html* (note the 'L' at the end). The fact that every user's home page has the same name is irrelevant, as each is in its own directory, and will be identified by its path. Exactly where your files will be stored is generally irrelevant. They will normally be somewhere on an FTP server, and when you log in to that server, it will take you directly to your directory.

Read their documentation, read their on-line help service (if any) and if that still doesn't tell you what you need to know, ring up and ask.

HTM and HTML

On the Unix systems that most service providers use, HTML documents are identified by the extension .HTML. On a PC, they are normally identified by the extension .HTM, though Windows 95 permits the use of .HTML.

Your service provider, like my local one at TCP, may insist that the home page document has an .HTML name, though subsidiary pages can have the .HTM extension. If this is the case, go through you pages now and edit any links back to the home page to add 'L' to the end of the name. You can change the home page's name when you upload it.

5.3 WS_FTP

This is the standard Windows application for handling your end of an FTP connection. If you do not have a copy, get one now. You can download it through your browser from the home site of its author (John Junod), at:

ftp://ftp2.ipswitch.com/pub/win32

or from any good shareware site. You can find it at:

http://www.shareware.com   (c|net shareware)

Windows 95 and Winsock

WS_FTP is available for Windows 95 and 3.1. The two versions have slight differences in their screen displays, but have the same set of commands and are used in the same ways.

The FTP connection

If you have used FTP before, it will probably have been to connect to one of the public FTP sites. With these, you log in as Anonymous, giving your e-mail name as a password. (WS_FTP will have collected this from you during installation, so you won't need to enter it for each new site.) Once at an FTP site you have limited access – downloading from public directories and uploading to designated incoming ones. You cannot normally create directories or rename or delete files. Logging in to your own directory on your provider's system is a different matter, as this is *your* place. You – and only you – have control here.

Accessing your Web space

Login to your service, then run WS_FTP. It should start with the Session Profile panel open. If it is not open, click the **Connect** button to open it.

Click **New**, then type in a **Profile name** for the connection – this can be anything that is meaningful to you.

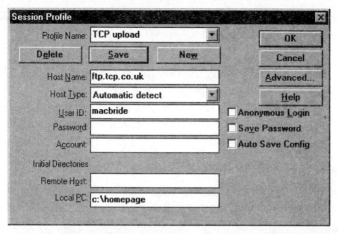

Don't forget to Save the Session profile after you have set it up!

For the **Host name**, enter the name of your provider's FTP server. The **User ID** is the same as the first part of your e-mail name.

Don't bother to enter your **Password**, it will be checked when you log in to your service provider's site.

You can change directory after you have logged in, but it is quicker and simpler to do it now. If you have been given the path to your directory at the service provider, enter it into the Remote Host slot. (Don't worry if you haven't been told – it almost certainly means you don't need to know.) Enter the path to the home page files' directory in the **Local PC** slot.

Make sure that you have entered the details correctly, then click **Save**. You will be needing this connection again.

Click **OK** to move to the main screen. You are ready to upload.

————— 5.4 Uploading —————

If everything is set up correctly, you should see a succession of messages scrolling through the narrow bottom pane of the WS_FTP window. Though some may be cryptic, and others move off before you have had a chance to read them, you should see enough to know that the conection is being made. You will know that you are there and ready to upload when you see your directory's name displayed at the *Remote System* slot at the top right of the window, and other activity ceases.

Select the files in your home page directory, and click [→] to send them to the remote system.

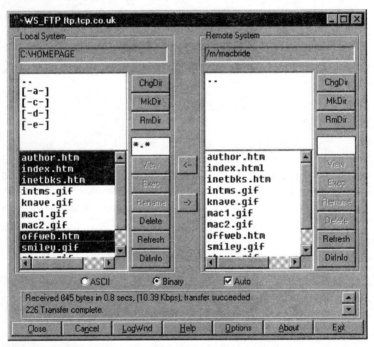

Using WS_FTP to upload edited pages and new files to the provider's system. Files are selected just as in File Manager or Explorer.

Before each file is sent, a panel will open, giving you a chance to change its name. This is the time to correct the extension to .HTML if necessary.

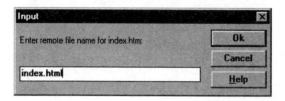

With larger files, you will see a Transfer Status panel open, displaying the progress of the uploading. HTML files are normally so small and transfer so quickly that all you see is a flash on the screen.

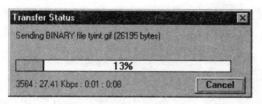

The whole set shouldn't take more than a few minutes to upload. After the last one has gone in, the directory listing on the Remote System pane will update. Check that they are all there, and if they are, click **Close** to shut down the FTP connection and click **Exit** to close WS_FTP.

—— 5.5 Uploading to CompuServe ——

If you are a CompuServe user, there is a special program – the Home Page Publishing Wizard – that handles uploading. Get a copy – it won't just make the process simple, it is the only way you can get your page on the Web!

Download a copy of the Wizard software either from the Internet section of CompuServe, through WinCIM, or by going to their Home page Web site at:

ourworld.compuserve.com

While you are there, you will also see their Home Page Wizard. This provides a simple, but restricted, means of producing home pages. We'll come back to that when we look at other HTML editors in Chapter 12.

The Publishing Wizard

This can be used both to upload new files and to delete ones that are already there. When you first start, you must tell it what you want to do.

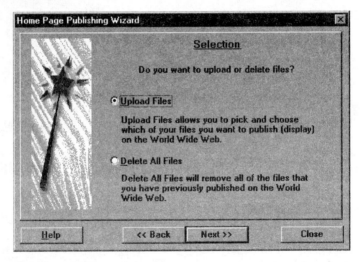

Select **Upload**, then click **Next** to move on. The next couple of pages are for your personal details – how much you want to make known is up to you. Do not feel that you have to give your occupation and interests, though including them makes it possible for other users, who share your interests, to contact you.

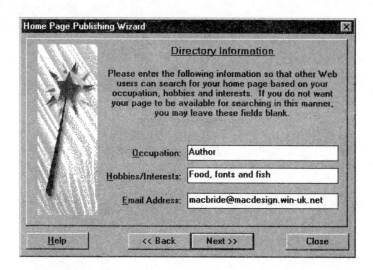

At the file selection window, switch to the right directory and select the files you want to upload. If you have been efficient, so that only home page files are there, you can click **Add All**.

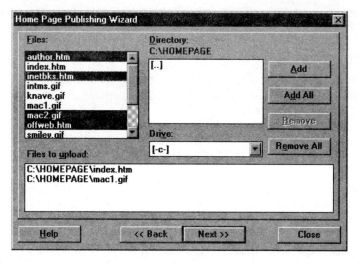

CompuServe does not insist on a standard name for the top level home page, but it does need to know which of the files to use as the top page of your system. Select it and click **Next**.

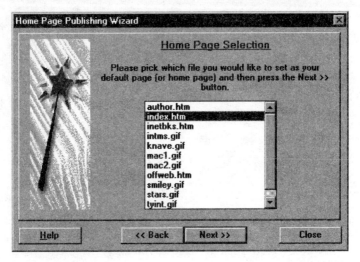

The Wizard finishes by checking your user number and password. It should have found these from your system, so that all you have to do is click **Next**. After that it will go on-line and load up your files for you.

The first time you use your CompuServe Web space, you will need to register a username. This becomes part of the URL of your page once it is in place.

KEEP TRYING!!

At the time of writing, it took enormous patience and perseverance to get the home page files up onto the Web – CompuServe's Web server was dropping connections faster than an arthritic waiter drops plates.

—— **5.6 Publishing from Navigator** ——

Netscape 3.0 (Gold) and Communicator have HTML editors (see
Chapter 12) to help you create your Web pages, and Publishing
facilities to simplify uploading.

Use the **File – Publish** command, or click the [Publish] icon to open
this dialog box.

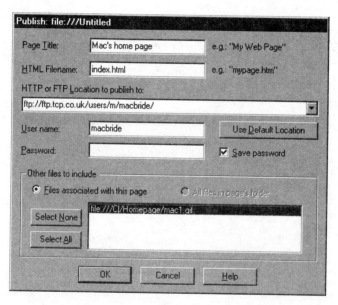

The essential information – filename, FTP location, your user
name and password – go into the top half of the dialog box.
Much of this information is stored, so that next time you will
only need to enter the page and filename (if different).

In the **Other files to include** area, you can select the graphics,
further pages for a multi-page set, and any other related files.
The first time that you upload, you would normally **Select All**.
When updating, you would only select new or changed files.

—— 5.7 Web publishing wizard ——

Internet Explorer users might like to get themselves a copy of Microsoft's Web publishing wizard – you'll find it in their free-stuff-to-download area.

There are several ways to use the wizard. This is probably the simplest way.

Locate all the files that you want to upload, and place them in a directory by themselves – if necessary make a new directory to hold them.

Contact your Internet Service Provider and find the URL of your Web space – this may be either an http:// or an ftp:// URL.

You are now ready to run smoothly through the wizard.

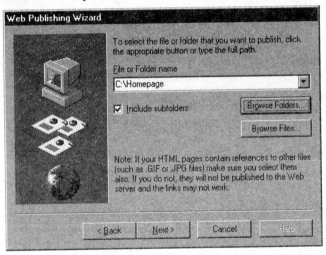

The first time that you use the Wizard, you will probably want to upload the whole set that makes up your home page system. Later, you will normally only be uploading any new and edited files. Moving these into a separate folder will make uploading easier – you can simply send the whole folder.

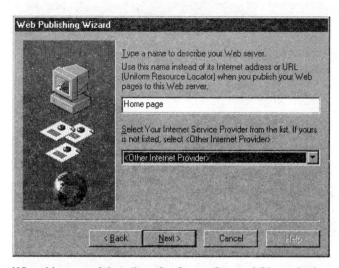

The Wizard has special routines for CompuServe, AOL, and other major providers. Users of other services have to do a little more work.

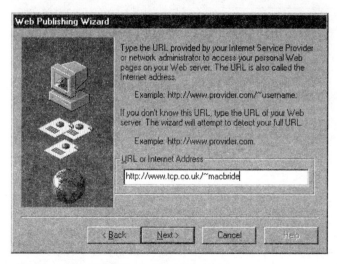

Your URL may be either ftp:// or http://

The Web publishing wizard can also be used for uploading pages within a company's network, as part of an intranet.

5.8 Testing

Your home page should be accessible from the Web within a few minutes of uploading your files. But where do you find it? Its URL will normally be the same as your service provider's, followed by a tilde (~) and your user name.

For example, my local provider's Web address is:

http://www.tcp.co.uk

my user name is macbride, and the URL for my page at TCP is:

http://www.tcp.co.uk/~macbride

Unless your service provider has told you otherwise, you can assume that the same pattern will work for you.

Run your browser, get on-line and use the Open Location command to go to your home page. Can you get there? If not, it may be that their system is a little slow on recognising the presence of new home page files.

Does it look as good on-line as it did during testing? Do the images download at a reasonable speed? Do the links all work? Remember that now you can test the links to other people's pages, FTP files, etc, as well as the links between your own pages.

Is it back to the drawing board, or is it time to let other people know that you are there?

———— 5.9 Publicity for your page ————

The key question here is 'Who do you want to visit you?'

If the aim is to make this a place for family and friends to drop in to pick up your latest news, then the best way to publicise your page is to ring them up and tell them that it's there.

If you have assembled links and information about your hobby or special interest, and would like to share this with fellow enthusiasts, then post an article in the relevant newsgroups announcing your arrival on the scene, (and hit the directories – see below).

If yours is a business home page, there may still be relevant newsgroups where an announcement would be welcomed, though this must be done thoughtfully. Some groups are distinctly non-commercial and do not appreciate business advertising – an announcement there could produce a flood of complaints in your e-mail. Some groups accept – and some are designed for – business home page announcements. Don't post to groups you don't know. Join and read enough of the articles in a newsgroup to get its flavour before you post to it.

If you are running an enthusiasts' resource page or a business page, or if you are a plain old-fashioned extrovert, *hit the directories*. There are several hundred directories on the Internet – large and small, specialised and general. Get your page into some or all of those and you should have visitors.

You can submit your page's URL to individual directories. The best way to do this is to go to the directory and look for a *Submit* sign. If you don't see one, they probably don't take unsolicited links. Amongst others, you might like to try:

Yahoo (www.yahoo.com),

Excite (www.excite.com)

The UK directory (www.ukdirectory.com).

The second approach is to use a promotion service. Submit It!, for instance, holds links to all the major Internet directories and search engines to which you can submit your URL. All you need to do is fill in one form, select which places you would like to have links to your page, then click the button to Submit It! Submit It! is at:

http://www.submit-it.com

Submit It! provides a one-stop approach to advertising your pages on the Web. It is well-organised and easy to use – try it.

————5.10 META and ISINDEX————

<META>

<META > tags go into the <HEAD> area, and are not visible on the page. They are mainly used to carry information about the page and its author. The basic shape is:

    <META NAME = ... VALUE = ...>

The NAME identifies the nature of the information, and the information itself is the VALUE. For example:

    <META NAME = author VALUE = "Ingrid Bottomlow">

If the VALUE contains more than one word, they should be enclosed in "quotes".

An important use for <META> tags – and why I have introduced them at this stage – is for carrying keywords. Some of the Internet's search engines will look for these and use them when compiling their databases. The tags should follow the pattern:

    <META NAME = keyword VALUE = "..." >

Keywords are not special words, simply ones that indicate the contents of your page. For example, the Cleethorpes Surfing Club home page might use this keyword tag:

    <META NAME = keyword VALUE = "surfing, water sports,
    North Sea, frostbite" >

<ISINDEX>

This provides another way to define words or phrases to be picked up by the search engines. Use it in the form:

    <ISINDEX PROMPT="Keywords">

The keywords are used in the same way as in the META tags.

5.11 Counters

If you would like to know how many people have visited your page, you can install a counter. For this you need a little assistance. You cannot actually count the number of visitors to your home page yourself, but there are a number of organisations on the Web that can do the counting for you. Their services are usually free – it is something they do to advertise their Web presence.

I got my counter from Net Digits, at:

http://www.digits.com

but the last time that I checked, they were not accepting new requests. WebTools, however, is providing counters. To get yours, head for their Counter page at:

http://www.webtools.org/counter

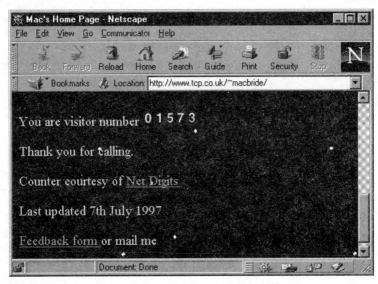

Come and see me – if only to boost my counter score!

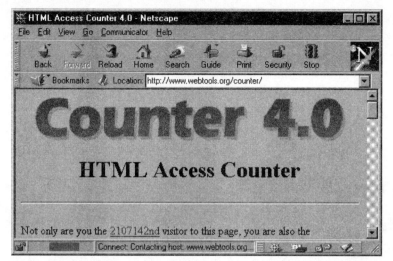

Go to WebTools to set up your counter – they make it easy to do.

Contact them when you have got your home page up and running successfully. There is a form to fill in, to give them the details of your page, and to set up your counter at their site.

The counter is given a name, which can be anything you like, e.g. 'maccount'. Once it has been created and its name confirmed, you can write a link to it into your home page.

The link is written into an <IMG SRC ...> tag, and should look something like this:

```
<IMG SRC = "http://counter.digits.com/wc/maccount">
```

Obviously, the URL will depend upon the counter service you use and the name you choose.

The counter can be embedded in some text:

```
You are visitor no. <IMG SRC = "http://counter.digits.com/wc/
maccount"> since 21st October 1997
```

These services ask their counter users to include a link to their page, as a trade-off for the free counting service. It is, anyway, a useful link, as they all do more than just supply counters.

―――――――――― **5.12 Summary** ――――――――――

● When preparing to upload, start by organising your HTML documents, graphics and any other related files into a single directory on your system.

● Test your system thoroughly before uploading – and pay special attention to the links between its pages.

● To upload your files to your service provider's computer, you will probably need WS_FTP.

● To upload to CompuServe, use their special Publishing Wizard.

● Netscape Gold and Communicator have a Publishing facility that simplifies uploading your files.

● You can download a Web publishing wizard from Microsoft. Though not quite as flexible as Netscape's publishing tool, it is easier to use than FTP.

● Once your Web page is in place, test it thoroughly, trying out every link.

● If a directory site has a '*Submit your URL*' (or similar) message, you can publicise your page there.

● If you go to Submit It! you can add your page to many directories and search engines.

● Keywords can be written into <META> and <ISINDEX> tags for the Internet's search engines to pick up.

● You can add a counter to your page by setting one up at an access counter service, such as Net Digits or WebTools.

6

LISTS AND LINES

6.1 Aims of this chapter

In this chapter we return to text, looking at two simple but effective ways to improve its appearance. If you want to display sets of links or other short items, they will look better as bulleted or numbered *lists*. If you want to divide your text into clearly marked sections, then *lines* can be drawn between them. Here we cover the tags and techniques that control these.

6.2 Lists

There are three types of lists – with bullets, with numbers or letters and lists of terms and definitions. For the first two types the techniques are the same, with the only difference being in the tags that define the list type. The default settings give you round bullets (●) and Arabic numerals (1,2,3), but options in the tags can be used to set a different bullet or numbering style.

Bulleted lists

A bulleted list is set up with the tag <UL> to mark its start and </UL> to close it.

Each item in the list is preceded by the tag <LI> (List Item). This needs no closing tag.

For example:

```
<HTML>
<H4>Our Gold Star service includes</H4>
<UL>
<LI>Free delivery
<LI>No quibble 'Return if not delighted'
<LI>Bio-degradable packaging
<LI>Special 2 for the price of one offer on Garlic bread
</UL>
</HTML>
```

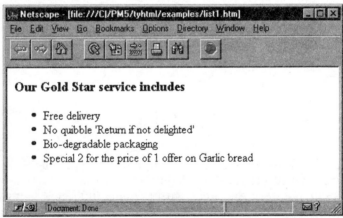

These items are all short enough to fit on single lines. If you have longer items, the continuation lines are also indented to match.

Variations

You will see that with a plain <UL> tag, the bullets are filled circles. If you prefer, you can add the phrase "TYPE = *keyword*", where the keyword is either SQUARE, DISC or CIRCLE.

SQUARE gives you a filled square;

DISC produces a filled circle – the default bullet;

CIRCLE, at the time of writing, produced an open square when viewed through Netscape. They may have got that bug sorted out by the time you read this!

If you like, you can include sub-headings within a list. Simply set one of the <H...> tags – choosing an appropriate level. It will be displayed as usual, though indented.

```
<HTML>
<H3>Our Gold Star service includes</H3>
<UL> TYPE = SQUARE>
<LI>Free delivery
<LI>No quibble 'Return if not delighted'
<LI>Bio-degradable packaging
<LI>Special 2 for the price of one offer on Garlic bread

<H4>Toppings</H4>

<LI>Pepperoni
<LI>Black Olives
<LI>Mushrooms
<LI>Ham and Pineapple
</UL>
</HTML>
```

Bullet type

Sub-heading

More list items

If you are sub-dividing your lists in this way, put extra blank lines into your code. They will make it easier to see the structure when you come back to edit it later.

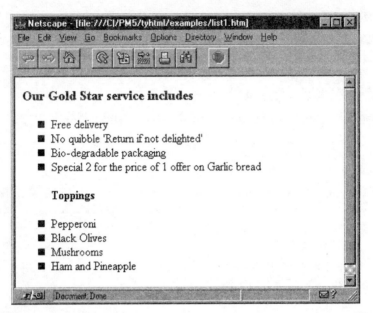

This is all one list. Notice that the 'Toppings' heading is indented to the same depth as the list items.

Nested lists

Lists can be 'nested', one inside the other, to give you several levels of indents. The same tags are used as for simple lists – but you must put a </UL> tag at the end of each inner level. Note that you can use different bullet styles for the inner and outer lists.

When writing nested lists, you will find it helpful to indent your inner list items in your code. It shows the structure more clearly, and it makes it easy to do a quick check that each opening <UL> tag has a matching </UL>.

Here are the 'Toppings' again, this time treated as a separate list, nested within the main Gold Star list:

```
<HTML>
<H3>Our Gold Star service includes</H3>
<UL TYPE = SQUARE>        _____ outer list start
<LI>Free delivery
<LI>No quibble 'Return if not delighted'
<LI>Bio-degradable packaging
<LI>Special 2 for the price of 1 offer on Garlic bread
<LI>With all your favourite toppings

    <UL TYPE = DISC>  _____ inner list start
    <LI>Pepperoni
    <LI>Black Olives
    <LI>Mushrooms            inner list items
    <LI>Ham and Pineapple
    </UL>  _____
                        inner list end
</UL>  _____
</HTML>        outer list end
```

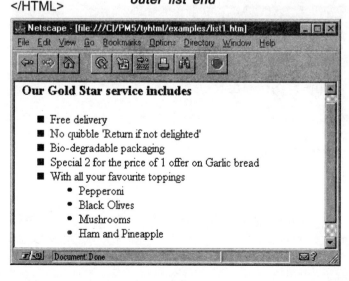

────────── **6.3 Numbered lists** ──────────

Numbered lists follow exactly the same rules as bulleted lists, but here the tag is <OL>.

If you do not specify the TYPE, you get Arabic (normal) numbers, as in this example:

```
<HTML>
<H2>Top 5 Directories</H2>
<OL>
<LI><A HREF = "http://www.yahoo.com">Browse at Yahoo</A>
<LI><A HREF = "http://www.lycos.com">Search at Lycos</A>
<LI><A HREF = "http://www.mckinley.com">Search at Magellan</A>
<LI><A HREF = "http://web2.pcwlink.com">PCW's Selection</A>
<LI><A HREF = "http://www.ukdirectory.co.uk">UK Directory</A>
</OL>
</HTML>
```

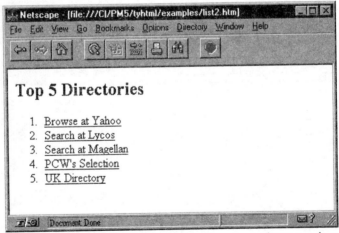

Plain Arabic numbers are the simplest to use, and can produce the clearest display.

If you want some variety – especially for nested lists – the TYPE options are 'I','i', 'A' and 'a'.

i   Roman numerals, i,ii,iii,iv
I   Roman capitals, I, II, III, IV
a   lower case letters a,b,c
A   capital letters, A, B, C

Here's an example of nested lists, using several of the TYPE options. It's from our friend Ingrid, who is having a busy day.

```
<HTML>

<H2>Things to do</H2>          — Level 1 list A,B,C
<OL TYPE = A>
<LI>Clean out the Guinea Pigs
    <OL TYPE = I>           Level 2 list, I, II, III
    <LI>Fetch the hay
    <LI>Push the pigs out of the way
    <LI>Shovel the old stuff where Pa won't fall in it
    </OL>                   End of level 2
<LI>Make some real bread
    <OL>                    Level 2 list, 1, 2, 3
    <LI>Buy some yeast          Level 3 list, i, ii, iii
        <OL TYPE = i>
        <LI>Try the village shop
        <LI>Try Seamus Sosmall
        </OL>              End of level 3
    <LI>Light the stove
    <LI>Get baking!
    </OL>                  End of level 2
</OL>                      End of level 1
</HTML>
```

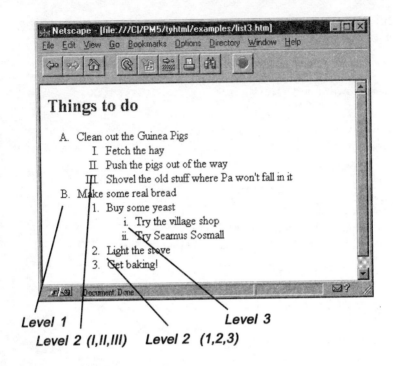

Level 1

Level 2 (I,II,III)   Level 2 (1,2,3)

Level 3

COMBINED STYLES

If you are nesting lists, you can use bullets for one level and numbers for another. A bulleted outer list and a numbered inner list can be a very effective combination. Don't forget that you can change the FONT SIZE, or use <B>, <I> and other highlighting tags to make some levels of text more or less prominent.

——————— 6.4 Definition lists ———————

These are ideally suited to lists of terms and definitions, but serve equally well for any set of text items where you want a series of sub-headings with following text. The tags used for these are:

<DL>   Marks the start of the list
<DT>   Identifies a term
<DD>   Identifies the definition
</DL>   Marks the end of the list

The <DL> and <DD> lines of text appear in the same font size and style – unless you specifically format them otherwise – but <DD> lines are indented one tab. The normal pattern is:

```
<DL>
     <DT>
     <DD>
     <DT>
     <DD>
     ...
</DL>
```

But there is nothing to stop you having several <DT> or <DD> tags in succession if you have a number of terms without definitions or several paragraphs of definition to one term. You can see this in the next example.

SPECIAL CHARACTERS

The symbols '**<**', '**>**', '**&**' and '**"**' have special meanings in HTML. If you want to use them in your text, you must substitute these expressions:

<	&lt (Less Than)	>	&gt (Greater Than)
&	&amp	"	&quot

Look out for them in the next example.

HTML>
<TITLE> Definition Lists </TITLE>
<H2> List tags </H2>
<DL>
<DT> &lt UL TYPE = square/disc/circle &gt
<DD> Marks the start of an Unordered (bulleted) list
<DT> &lt OL TYPE = i/I/a/A &gt
<DD> Marks the start of an Ordered (numbered/lettered) list
<DT> &lt DL &gt
<DD> Marks the start of a Definition list.
<DD> This takes no options ⎯⎯   *<DD> for second definition*
<DT> &lt LI &gt
<DT> &lt /DL &gt   ↘ *2 <DT>'s without definitions*
</HTML>

This definition list defines list tags! Notice how the '&lt' and '&gt' expressions have been displayed as symbols.

—————— 6.5 Fancy bullets ——————

Bored with blobs in your lists? You can create fancy bulleted
'lists' by fitting your own bullet images at the starts of lines.
These won't be proper lists, as defined by <OL> or <UL> tags,
but they will look good on screen. It is a bit more work, as you
have to make the bullets and set the indents – which is, in effect,
what the list tags do for you – but the results are worthwhile.

Create the bullet image in Paint. If your drawing skills are not
too hot, then use a Wingding character – 24 point is a good size.
Select the image, and use **Edit|Copy To...** to save it to file.
Use Lview or PaintShop to convert this to a GIF file, and save it
in your HTML directory.

*Here I have used Wingding 'J' for the image. At this point, it has just
been selected and is about to be saved as a BMP file.*

Now to build the list. There are three things to bear in mind:

- We need an image at the start of every item line.
- To create an indent, we will need to set the HSPACE value in the <IMG SRC ...> tag.
- The lines of item text must be separated – and <BR> will give a shallower break than <P>.

The resulting source code is nothing like as compact as an <OL> or <UL> list, but the display is better.

In this example, I have also replaced the top heading with a graphic.

```
<HTML>
<BODY BGCOLOR = FFFFFF>
<CENTER><IMG SRC = "top5head.gif" ALT = "Top 5
Directories"></CENTER>          HSPACE to indent the text

<IMG SRC = "redbtn.gif" ALIGN = TOP HSPACE = 20><A
HREF = "http://www.yahoo.com">Browse at Yahoo</A>
<BR> ———————————— Use <P> for deeper spacing
<IMG SRC = "redbtn.gif" ALIGN = TOP HSPACE = 20><A
HREF = "http://www.lycos.com">Search at Lycos</A>
<BR>
<IMG SRC = "redbtn.gif" ALIGN = TOP HSPACE = 20><A
HREF = "http://www.mckinley.com">Search at Magellan</A>
<BR>
<IMG SRC = "redbtn.gif" ALIGN = TOP HSPACE = 20><A
HREF = "http://web2.pcwlink.com/favorite.html">PCW's
Selection</A>
<BR>
<IMG SRC = "redbtn.gif" ALIGN = TOP HSPACE = 20><A
HREF = "http://www.ukdirectory.co.uk">UK Directory</A>
</BODY>
</HTML>
```

Bullets like this are very small files – under 1Kb – so download quickly. Most visitors will wait a few seconds to get a brighter display.

——————— 6.6 Line styles ———————

The basic <HR> line is two pixels deep, stretches more or less the full width of the window, and has a shaded effect. These aspects can all be changed by options in the <HR> tag.

SIZE = *value*

This sets the thickness of the line, counting in pixels. The SIZE must be at least 2 if you want a shade effect. Over about 8 pixels, it looks less like a line than a box.

WIDTH = *value*

This sets the width of the line. As with the WIDTH option of images, you can either count in pixels or set it to a percentage of the browser window's width. Unless you want the line to match a heading or image, or you are creating a pattern of lines, it is usually best to set the width as a percentage. You then get the same effect, whatever size window it is viewed in.

ALIGN = *value*

This sets the line to the left, right or in the centre of the screen. It can only be used if the width has been set.

NOSHADE

If this keyword is used, the line is shown as a plain dark line.

You can see the effect of setting the SIZE and (pixel) WIDTH in this example. Try it for yourself – and with other values.

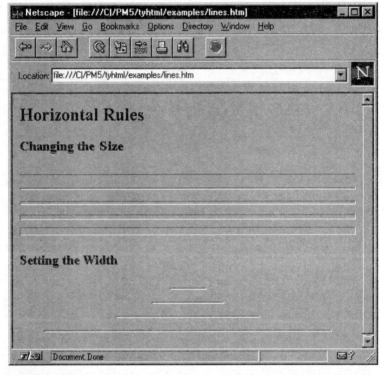

That first line in the Size set is only 1 pixel deep – note that it has not been shaded. In the Width set, the first two lines (50 and 100 pixels) are too small to be significant if used alone, but could be combined with longer lines to good effect.

```
<HTML>
<H2> Horizontal Rules </H2>

<H3>Changing the Size</H3>
<HR SIZE = 1>
<HR SIZE = 2>
<HR SIZE = 4>
<HR SIZE = 6>
<HR SIZE = 10>

<H3>Setting the Width</H3>
<HR WIDTH = 50>
<HR WIDTH = 100>
<HR WIDTH = 200>
<HR WIDTH = 400>
</HTML>
```

This next example brings in the ALIGN and NOSHADE keywords, sets WIDTH in percentages and also applies several settings to some lines.

```
<HTML>
<H3>Alignment</H3>
<HR WIDTH = 40% ALIGN = left>
<HR SIZE = 6 WIDTH = 60% ALIGN = center>
<HR WIDTH = 40% ALIGN = right>

<H3>Shade or NOSHADE</H3>
<HR SIZE = 4 WIDTH = 80>
<HR SIZE = 4 WIDTH = 80 NOSHADE>
</HTML>
```

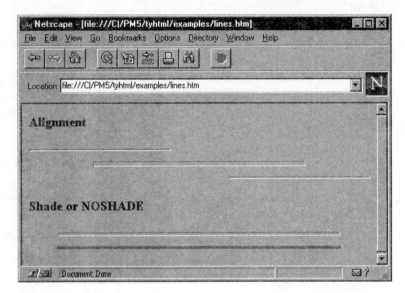

I don't know about you, but I prefer the standard 3-D shaded lines to the NOSHADE effect. I think we'll forget that option.

———— 6.7 Graphic lines ————

For a really different divider, create a slim graphic, and place that in your document instead of an <HR> line.

Set the image in <CENTER> tags, and use <P> either side for good spacing from the surrounding text. For example:

```
<P> <CENTER><IMG SRC = "lineimg.gif"> </CENTER> <P>
```

You can also use an image to create vertical lines in the background – a thickish bar of contrasting colour down the left edge can be very effective. The image does not need to be a large one. As HTML automatically repeats any background image to fill the screen, all that is essential is that the graphic is too wide to be repeated across the screen.

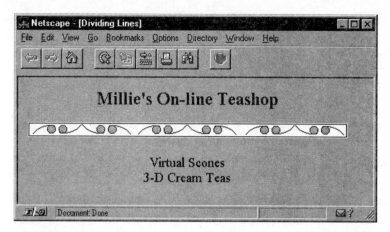

Add a little tone to your page with a tasteful decorated divider! This one was created in Paint, but DTP packages can be a good source of decorated lines if you do not want to make your own.

Vertical lines can make an effective background. The images used for this and the divider were both less than 1Kb – adding little to downloading time.

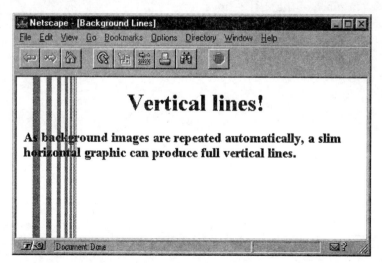

6.8 Summary

- Sets of short items can be neatly presented as lists.

- Lists can be nested inside one another, and headings can be used within lists.

- The <UL> tag creates bulleted lists. Its TYPE option gives you a limited choice of bullet styles.

- Ordered lists, set up with the <OL> tag, can have Roman or Arabic numbers or lower case or capital letters.

- Definition lists were designed for terms and definitions, but suit any data where a sub-heading is to be followed by plain text.

- You can inset images into lists, to act as bullets.

- The <HR> tag can take several options to define the size and nature of the line.

- Images can be droppped into your page to act as dividers, in place of the <HR> lines.

7

FORMS

7.1 Aims of this chapter

HTML forms provide a simple means for your visitors to contact you, to give you feedback on your page or to request further details of your products. They look very like ordinary paper-based forms and can be treated by your visitors in much the same way. Unlike paper forms, however, these can be sent by clicking on a button. In this chapter we will construct several forms, starting with simple text-only entries, and later adding checkboxes, radio buttons and drop-down lists.

FORMS AND BROWSERS

Forms were introduced in HTML 2.0, so anyone using an old browser will not be able to view your forms, or send you information through them. As I suspect that few people are still using pre-HTML 2.0 browsers, this shouldn't be a major problem, but it might be worth including "e-mail me for details" alternative, if you are very keen to get feedback.

——————— 7.2 The basic form ———————

Unlike other aspects of HTML, forms involve two-way communication, and they will only function if your service provider is able to process the incoming data. This should not create a problem – in essence all they have to do is run some standard software to pick up the feedback from your visitors. If your service provider cannot handle the feedback from forms, give them a nudge.

A form can be written on a page of its own, or be included within a larger page. It can include the normal range of text, lists, images, links and other objects, but it can also include the tags that will collect data and send the form.

The start of the form is marked by the <FORM> tag, and will contain the two keywords METHOD and ACTION. These can each take several options, and the simplest is this:

    <FORM METHOD = Post ACTION = mailto:your_address>

With these settings, the data entered into the form is e-mailed to you when the form is submitted – though only from Netscape! If you want feedback from all your readers, you need to use a CGI script (see page 127).

Within the form, data is collected mainly in <INPUT ...>tags. There are a number of options that can be used here. The most important is NAME = ... which sets up a *variable* – a place to store data input by your visitor.

    <INPUT NAME = email>

This creates the variable *email*. It will be displayed on screen as a blank data entry slot, 20 characters wide. For a different size slot, add the option SIZE = ..., giving the number of characters.

Put some text nearby, so your visitors know what it is for:

    E-mail address: <INPUT NAME = email SIZE = 30>

A second option that you must know about is one that sets up a button to send the form's contents back to you. The basic shape:

    <INPUT TYPE = Submit VALUE = "Send Now">

The phrase:

    TYPE = Submit

defines it as a button that submits feedback. The similar phrase:

    TYPE = Reset

defines a button to clear the form's contents.

    VALUE = "Send Now"

defines the button's caption. You can use any text you like, but you must enclose it in quotes or only the first word will be displayed.

Using only what we have covered so far, we can produce this simple feedback form:

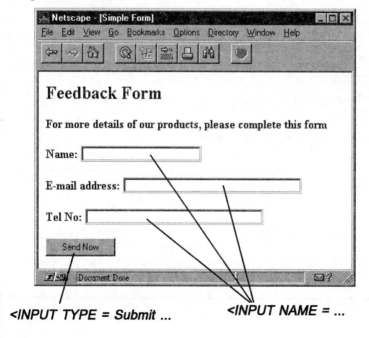

<INPUT TYPE = Submit ...   <INPUT NAME = ...

```
<HTML>
<TITLE> Simple Form </TITLE>
<H2> Feedback Form </H2>                    Start of Form
<FORM METHOD = Post ACTION =
mailto:macbride@tcp.co.uk>                  Your e-mail address
<B>
For more details of our products, please complete this form <P>
Name: <INPUT NAME = Surname> <P>
E-mail address: <INPUT NAME = Email SIZE = 30> <P>
Tel No: <INPUT NAME = Phone SIZE = 30> <P>
<INPUT TYPE = Submit VALUE = "Send Now">
</B>
</FORM>                          Closing tag for Form area
</HTML>
```

When someone submits your form, it is mailed to you automatically. When you next check your mailbox, you will find an entry labelled 'Form posted from Mozilla'. Read it, and you will find an attachment. Look at that and you will see something like this:

Surname=Bill+Gates&Email=bgates@microsoft.com&Phone=...

Not the clearest way to present information, is it? We will look at analysing returns in section 7.7.

BUSINESS FEEDBACK

If you are marketing a busines on the Web, and expect lots of feedback, talk to your service provider. Most can set things up so that replies are collected, collated into a more useable form and mailed out once a day.

—7.3 Feedback from CGI scripts—

We noted earlier that the ACTION = mailto: ... method only
works if your visitors are using Netscape. If your visitors are
browsing with Internet Explorer, clicking **Submit** simply starts
up the New Mail Message routine – and data entered into the
form is discarded. If you want all your visitors to be able to mail
the form, and not just the 80% or so Netscape users, you need to
use a CGI script. And for this you need the co-operation of your
service provider.

CGI is a programming language, devised for use on the Internet.
Its scripts (programs) can only be run on suitable servers, such
as the computers at your service provider. Most providers have
several ready-made ones that you can use, and amongst these
there should be one which will handle feedback from forms. The
scripts are normally straightforward to use – a few adjustments
to your form should be all that is needed.

Here is how you would use the feedback script at my service,
Total Connectivity Providers. Theirs is the *formmail* script, by
Matt Wright. Yours may use the same one, or something similar
– but check with them before you go much further.

The <FORM ACTION... line calls up the script:

```
<FORM ACTION = "http://www.tcp.co.uk/cgi-bin/formmail"
METHOD = "POST">
```

Within the form, you must have a *recipient* field, which holds
your e-mail address, so that the script knows where to mail the
feedback. You don't want this to appear on the form, so it must
be hidden. Here's what the line should look like:

```
<INPUT TYPE = "hidden" NAME = "recipient" VALUE =
"macbride@tcp.co.uk">
```

Your form will almost certainly include fields for your visitor's
e-mail address and real name. If you would like this information
to be included in the From: line of the message, when the script
mails it to you, those fields should be called *email* and *realname*.

```
<P>Name: <INPUT TYPE = text NAME = "realname">
<P>E-mail address:
<INPUT TYPE = text NAME = "email" SIZE = 30>
```

The rest of the form is identical, whether it is being returned to you by a ACTION=mailto: or by a CGI script.

CHECK THE SCRIPT

Do check with your service provider before starting on this. It is possible that they do not have a facility for running scripts, and even more likely that their scripts are used differently.

7.4 Checkboxes and radios

If you want your form-fillers to be able to choose from a set of alternatives, you should use the TYPE options:

☑ Checkbox where several alternatives can be chosen, or

◉ Radio, where only one of the set can be selected

They are used in very similar ways, with one significant exception. With checkboxes, each INPUT should have its own NAME variable, to store the response.

```
I am interested in: <BR>
<INPUT TYPE = Checkbox NAME = hard> Hardware <BR>
<INPUT TYPE = Checkbox NAME = soft> Software <BR>
<INPUT TYPE = Checkbox NAME = books> Books <P>
```

If the visitor selects the *Hardware* checkbox, the variable *hard* will have the value *on*.

With radio buttons, the same NAME should be used for all the radios in the set, as you only want to allow one of the alternatives to be chosen:

Sex:

<INPUT TYPE = Radio NAME = sex VALUE = m CHECKED> Male

<INPUT TYPE = Radio NAME = sex VALUE = f > Female <P>

<INPUT TYPE = Radio NAME = sex VALUE = dk> Don't Know <P>

We now need to add the VALUE = clause. This sets the value to be returned, so that the feedback will be in the form of *sex = dk* (if you have an indecisive visitor). If you omit the VALUE =, the feedback would read *sex = on*, whatever was selected.

Notice the keyword CHECKED in the first <INPUT... above. This sets the default. Miss it out if you want to start with all the radios clear.

Compare this screen display with the following HTML code.

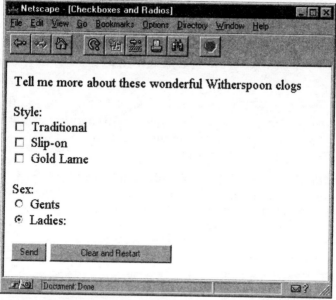

This form also has a TYPE = Reset button to clear the form, in case the visitor wants to start again.

```
<HTML>
<FORM METHOD = Post ACTION = mailto:sales@clogs.co.uk>

Tell me more about these wonderful Witherspoon clogs <P>
Style: <BR>
<INPUT TYPE = Checkbox NAME = trad> Traditional <BR>
<INPUT TYPE = Checkbox NAME = slipon> Slip-on <BR>
<INPUT TYPE = Checkbox NAME = gold> Gold Lame <P>
Sex: <BR>
<INPUT TYPE = Radio NAME = sex VALUE = m > Gents <BR>
<INPUT TYPE = Radio NAME = sex VALUE = f CHECKED>
Ladies <P>
<INPUT TYPE = Submit VALUE = "Send">
<INPUT TYPE = Reset VALUE = "Clear and Restart">

</FORM>
</HTML>
```

———————— **7.4 Text areas** ————————

The simple <INPUT ...> only accepts one line of text. If you
wanted to collect your visitor's (snail mail) address, you would
have to use several of those, or one of these:

```
<TEXTAREA NAME = Address>
```

This displays as a small box with scroll bars to the right and
bottom. It really is small. For most practical purposes you would
want to make it into a decent size by adding the options ROWS
and COLS to define the size of the display. The one in the
screenshot below was produced by these lines:

```
Address: <BR>
<TEXTAREA NAME = Address ROWS = 4 COLS = 40>
</TEXTAREA>
```

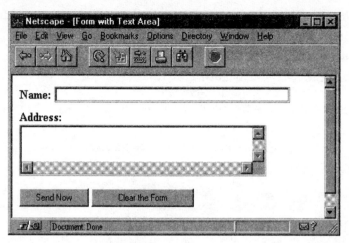

Three things to note here.

● The <BR> after the prompt text places it above the text area. If you miss this out, to put the prompt to the left, it aligns with the bottom of the text area and looks a mess.
● The ROWS and COLS settings only affect the display size. If your visitors want to write more lines, or longer ones, they can– that's what the scroll bars are there for.
● <TEXTAREA ...> needs a closing </TEXTAREA> tag.

─────── 7.5 Drop-down lists ───────

Drop-down lists are one of the neatest ways of offering a set of alternatives. In HTML they can be implemented with the tags <SELECT ...> and <OPTION = ...>

<SELECT ...> provides the framework for the list. It takes the keyword NAME to define the variable where the selection will be recorded. The matching tag </SELECT> closes the list.

<OPTION = ...> defines an entry for the list. It must have a word inside the tag – this will be fed back to you in the SELECT

NAME variable – and a label to go on the list. You need an
<OPTION = ...> tag for every item.

The tags fit together like this:

```
<SELECT NAME = Level>
   <OPTION = stand> Standard
   <OPTION = prof> Professional
</SELECT>
```

That gives us a drop down list with two items.

If the visitor selects *Standard*, the *stand* option will be passed
to *Level*, and the feedback mail will include this phrase:

```
Level = stand
```

An <OPTION = ...> tag can include the word SELECTED, to set
that item as the default.

Look for the line:

```
<OPTION = Win SELECTED> PC/Windows
```

in this next example, and notice how the item *PC/Windows* is
displayed at the top of the list, in the selection slot – though its
natural place is further down.

```
<HTML>
<H2> Order Form </H2>

<FORM METHOD = Post ACTION = mailto:sales@pcs.co.uk>
Order your software here: <P>
Platform: <SELECT NAME = Platform>            Prompt
   <OPTION = Pcdos > PC/DOS
   <OPTION = Mac> Mac
   <OPTION = Unix> Unix
   <OPTION = Win SELECTED> PC/Windows
</SELECT>
```

```
Level: <SELECT NAME = Level>
   <OPTION = stand> Standard
   <OPTION = prof> Professional
</SELECT>
<P>
<INPUT TYPE = Submit VALUE = "Send" >
</FORM>
</HTML>
```

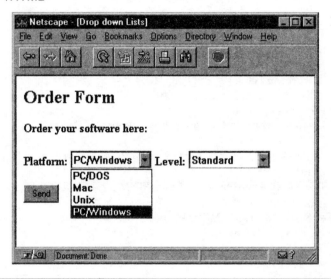

PROMPTS

Never leave your visitors guessing. Always include a prompt, even if you think that a select list should be self-explanatory. Your visitors can ignore prompts that they don't need, but they cannot read your mind. In the example given here, the prompts are very brief, and the forms would be more user-friendly if they had a little more in the way of helpful text.

—— 7.6 A full featured form ——

Let's tie all these <INPUT ...> tags together in one form, then take a good look at the data that is returned from it.

The form, shown opposite, includes a <TEXTAREA ...> for the visitor's address, checkboxes, radios and a <SELECT ...> list for their choices of options. Here's the code:

```
<HTML>
<TITLE>Full Feature Form</TITLE>
<BODY BGCOLOR = FFFFFF TEXT = 000000>

<FORM METHOD = Post ACTION =
mailto:sales@artpacks.co.uk>
<H2>On-Line Art Packs</H2>
Please send me information about your Art Collections
<P>
Name: <INPUT NAME = contact SIZE = 30> <BR>
Address: <BR>
<TEXTAREA NAME = Address ROWS = 4 COLS = 40>
</TEXTAREA> <BR>
Tel No: <INPUT NAME = Phone> <BR>
E-mail: <INPUT NAME = email SIZE = 30>
<P>
I am interested in: <BR>
<INPUT TYPE = Checkbox NAME = clip> Clip Art <BR>
<INPUT TYPE = Checkbox NAME = paint> Paintings <BR>
<INPUT TYPE = Checkbox NAME = photo> Photographs
<P>
Computer: <SELECT NAME = computer>
    <OPTION = Amiga> Amiga
    <OPTION = Arch> Archimedes
    <OPTION = Mac> Mac
    <OPTION = Pcdos > PC/DOS
    <OPTION = Unix> Unix
    <OPTION = Win SELECTED> PC/Windows
</SELECT>
```

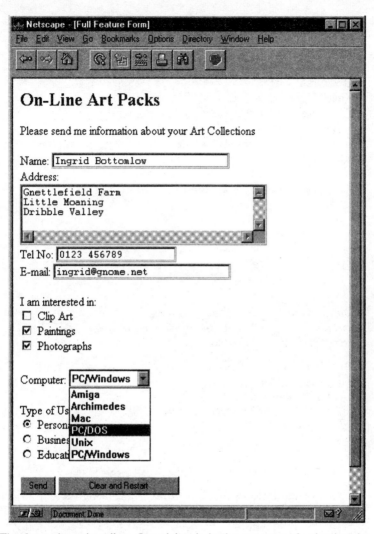

The form viewed on-line. Our visitor is in the process of selecting the computer type. Refer back to this when you get to the analysis in the next section.

```
<P>Type of Use: <BR>
<INPUT TYPE = Radio NAME = usage VALUE = pers>
Personal <BR>
<INPUT TYPE = Radio NAME = usage VALUE = bus>
Business <BR>
<INPUT TYPE = Radio NAME = usage VALUE = educ>
Educational <BR>
<INPUT TYPE = Submit VALUE = "Send">
<INPUT TYPE = Reset VALUE = "Clear and Restart">
</FORM>

<A HREF = index.htm> Return to the top page </A>
</HTML>
```

——— 7.7 Analysing returns ———

If you get your form feedback from a CGI script, it will normally be in plain text or HTML format – ready to read. If it is sent back by Netscape's **mailto**, it will not be quite so readable.

Each of the NAME variables is followed by whatever your visitor typed in, though spaces will have been turned into '+' signs, and some symbols will have been replaced by code numbers – in this example '/' in 'PC/DOS' has become '%2F'. This is hexadecimal for 47, and the ASCII code number for '/'.

The variables are separated from each other by '&' signs.

Here's the feedback from Ingrid's visit to the last form:

```
contact=Ingrid+Bottomlow&Address=Gnettlefield+Farm%0D%0A
Little+Moaning%0D%0ADribble+Valley&Phone=0123+456789
&email=ingrid@gnome.net&paint=on&photo=on&computer=
PC%2FDOS&usage=pers
```

It wouldn't take much to write a little program or a macro to convert this to a more usable form.

We could use a word-processor to make these these replacements:

Find	Replace with
&	new paragraph
%0D%0A	comma
+	space

It now reads:

```
contact=Ingrid Bottomlow
Address=Gnettlefield Farm, Little Moaning, Dribble Valley
Phone=0123 456789
email=ingrid@gnome.net
paint=on
photo=on
computer=PC/DOS
usage=pers
```

From this, we can tell that Ms Bottomlow is interested in the Painting and Photograph collections (both set to *on*), but not Clip Art – if the variable is not *on*, it is not included in the feedback. She has also selected the *PC/DOS* option from the *computer* list, and the *pers* radio button in the *usage* set.

7.8 Summary

- Forms are supported by all modern browsers, though if you wanted to guarantee that your visitors could get data to you, you should provide a simple e-mail alternative.

- At the start of every form, set the METHOD = to Post and give your e-mail address in the ACTION= option, to get feedback posted to you.

- CGI scripts will give more reliable feedback of form data. Your service provider should have ready-made scripts that you can use to get feedback.

- If an <INPUT ...> tag is to return a value, it must have a variable defined by NAME =.

- You can set the SIZE option to fix the width of the data entry slot.

- <INPUT TYPE = Checkbox will create a tickable checkbox on screen. These can be used where multiple selections can be made.

- <INPUT TYPE = Radio creates a radio button. Sets of radio buttons should share a NAME variable, but each have their own VALUE.

- For multi-line text data entry, use a <TEXTAREA ...> tag, setting the ROWS and COLS options if you want to fix their displayed size.

- Drop-down lists can be created with the <SELECT ...> and <OPTION ...> tags.

- The feedback from forms is not particularly easy to read, but a few minutes' search-and-replace in a wordprocessor will give you clear results.

8

TABLES

HTML 3.0

8.1 Aims of this chapter

One of the most compact and readable ways of displaying items
of information is in a table. They are fiddly to construct, but
well worth the effort in their impact. Here we start with very
simple tables, and gradually add features.

8.2 The use of tables

Tables can be used to display text, links, graphics or any other
items that can go anywhere else on a Web page. They may be
any size from a couple of items in a single row, up to half a
dozen or more columns and dozens of rows. They can be used
simply as a means of presenting information, or can be so
enhanced with borders, colours and graphics that they become
decorative items in their own right.

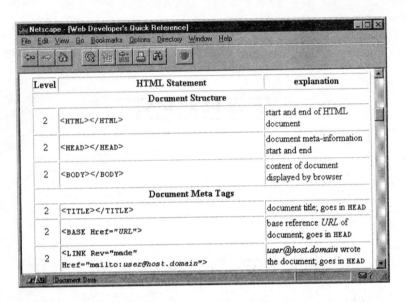

Level	HTML Statement	explanation
Document Structure		
2	`<HTML></HTML>`	start and end of HTML document
2	`<HEAD></HEAD>`	document meta-information start and end
2	`<BODY></BODY>`	content of document displayed by browser
Document Meta Tags		
2	`<TITLE></TITLE>`	document title; goes in HEAD
2	`<BASE Href="URL">`	base reference *URL* of document; goes in HEAD
2	`<LINK Rev="made" Href="mailto:user@host.domain">`	*user@host.domain* wrote the document; goes in HEAD

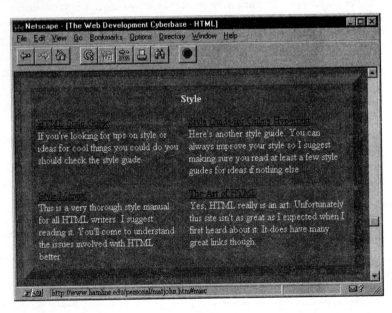

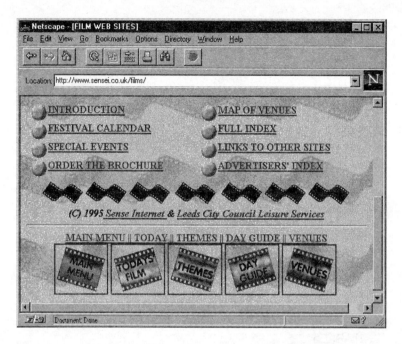

The three screenshots on these pages show some of the effects you can achieve with tables.

Top left: *John December's Web Developer's Quick Reference uses a clear and simple design that is very easy to read.*

Bottom left: *Mat John's Web Development Cyberbase goes in for an unusual range of colours and bold, raised borders. Notice that the items in the tables each have a header line and text – a table entry is not restricted to a single piece of text.*

Above: *This set of bulleted links in Leeds City Council's Film Festival page is scarcely recognisable as a table, but it is. Graphics can be used in tables, with or without accompanying text.*

———————— 8.3 The basic tags ————————

For a simple table, you only need three pairs of tags, used in this pattern:

```
<TABLE>
<TR>
<TD> Column item  </TD>
<TD> Column item </TD>
... across the columns
</TR>
<TR>
<TD> Column item  </TD>
... across the columns
</TR>
... down all the rows
</TABLE>
```

The table is built from the top left, working across the columns. Each item is enclosed in <TD> </TD> tags, and each row is enclosed in <TR> </TR> tags. It takes a lot of tags to make a big table!

Drawing up a rough sketch first helps to get the coding right. For instance, suppose we wanted a table of the Elements (the alchemists', not the modern one – that's too big for us!). Here's our sketch:

Earth	Air
Fire	Water

The first row has two items – 'Earth' and 'Air', the second second has 'Fire' and 'Water'. That give us this HTML code:

```
<HTML>
<TABLE>
   <TR>
         <TD> Earth </TD>
         <TD> Air </TD>
   </TR>
   <TR>
         <TD> Fire </TD>
         <TD> Water </TD>
   </TR>
</TABLE>
</HTML>
```

Notice that I have indented each row by one tab space, and each item by a second. This is not essential, but it makes the document more readable and easier to check – you can simply run your finger down the page making sure than each <TR> has its matching </TR>.

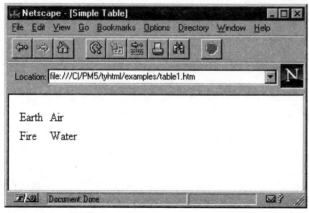

Not very impressive, but it's a start!

That wasn't much to write home about, was it. Let's try again. This time, we will put two lines of text in each place in the table, setting the top line in <B> to make it into a header.

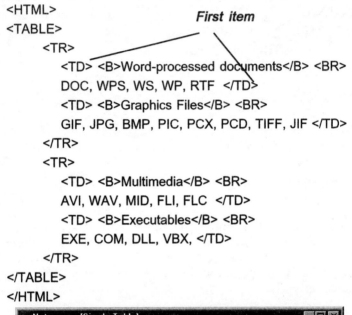

```
<HTML>                          First item
<TABLE>
    <TR>
        <TD> <B>Word-processed documents</B> <BR>
        DOC, WPS, WS, WP, RTF  </TD>
        <TD> <B>Graphics Files</B> <BR>
        GIF, JPG, BMP, PIC, PCX, PCD, TIFF, JIF </TD>
    </TR>
    <TR>
        <TD> <B>Multimedia</B> <BR>
        AVI, WAV, MID, FLI, FLC  </TD>
        <TD> <B>Executables</B> <BR>
        EXE, COM, DLL, VBX, </TD>
    </TR>
</TABLE>
</HTML>
```

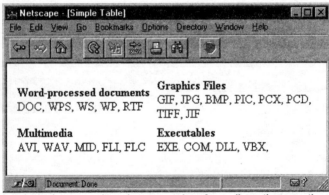

Notice that where one item in a row takes fewer lines than another, the lines are in the middle of the vertical space.

8.4 Borders

Adding a border is very easy and greatly improves the look of tables. At the simplest, it is just a matter of including the keyword BORDER in the <TABLE> tag. Here is the same table with the tag edited to read:

```
<TABLE BORDER>
```

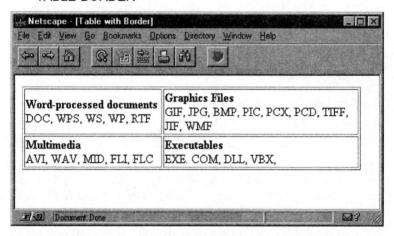

The default settings are to have each item bordered by a thin line, a slim border around the whole table, a narrow space between the inner and outer borders, and the text close to the edge of the inner borders.

The latter three settings can be changed.

BORDER can take a value, setting its width in pixels, e.g.:

```
BORDER = 10
```

CELLSPACING = ... sets the distance, in pixels, between the inner and outer borders

CELLPADDING = ... sets the distance, in pixels, between the inner border and the text.

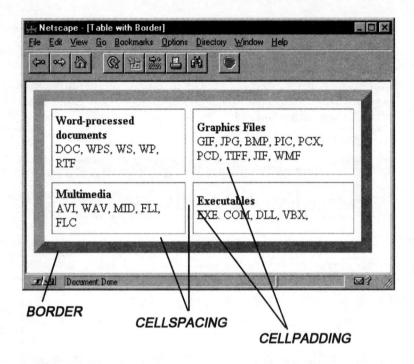

Here is the table again, this time with all three options set in the <TABLE ...> tag:

`<TABLE BORDER = 15 CELLSPACING = 10 CELLPADDING = 5>`

HIDING INNER BORDERS

The border colours are set automatically to contrast with the background. However, if you set a BODY BGCOLOR value that uses only half-beam colours, e.g. "808000", "008000" or "808080", the inner borders disappear!

——— 8.5 Headings and captions ———

Tables normally need some form of headings to explain what they are about.

<CAPTION>

Use this to add a (bold) caption to the table. It is normally placed above it, but you can use the option *ALIGN = Bottom* to place it below. The caption text must be closed with </CAPTION>.

<TH>

This marks a heading, to a row or column within the table. It is used like a <TD> tag, but sets the text in bold and aligns it in the centre of its cell. Close the heading with a </TH> tag.

This can take options to make the heading span more than one row or column. We will return to these in section 8.6.

As usual, it helps if you plan ahead. Here's a sketch of the table that I want to build.

	Florida	Malaga	Tuscany
7 nights	£479	£399	£359
14 nights	£629	£519	£539

The table will have three rows and four columns. The top row will have four <TH> tags, including an empty one at the start to create that blank cell in the top left. The other two rows will each have one <TH> followed by three <TD> tags.

```
<HTML>
<TITLE> Table with Headings</TITLE>
<BODY BGCOLOR = FFFFFF TEXT = 000000>
<TABLE BORDER = 5 cellspacing = 5 cellpadding = 5 >

<CAPTION>
<H3>Up and Away Holidays</H3>
</CAPTION>
   <TR>
        <TH>  </TH>
        <TH> Florida </TH>
        <TH> Malaga </TH>
        <TH> Tuscany </TH>
   </TR>
   <TR>
        <TH> 7 nights </TH>
        <TD> £479 </TD>
        <TD> £399 </TD>
        <TD> £359 </TD>
   </TR>
   <TR>
        <TH> 14 nights </TH>
        <TD> £629 </TD>
        <TD> £519 </TD>
        <TD> £539 </TD>
   </TR>
</TABLE>
</BODY>
</HTML>
```

Captions are normally in the standard font size

Blank cell

Column headers

Row header

FONTS IN TABLES

If you want to change the font of headings or entries in tables, you must write a <H ...> or <FONT SIZE ...> tag within the <TH> or <TD> tag for each item. You cannot set a size or style to apply to the whole table.

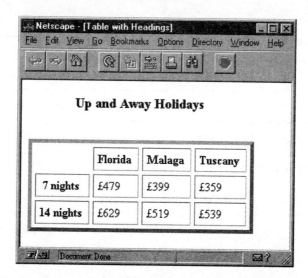

Note that the blank <TH> tag produces an unbordered space, rather than an empty cell. Setting the caption as a <H3> heading has forced a space beneath it. If we had used <FONT SIZE ...>, it could have been kept closer to the table.

8.6 Irregular grids

Not all tables fit into a simple grid. With some you will want two or more levels of headings, with category headings in one row spanning a set of headings in the row below; an item within the table may apply to several rows and/or columns.

Both <TH> headings and <TD> items can be extended across or down the cells with the options:

ROWSPAN =   to set the number of rows deep

COLSPAN =   to set the number of columns across

Let's extend that last table, starting as before with a sketch.

Up and Away Holidays

2 Rows x 2 Cols   *2 Columns*

		US	Europe	
		Florida	Malaga	Tuscany
7 nights	Full Board	£479	£399	£359
14 nights	Full Board	£629	£519	£539
	Self-Catering	£529	£419	

2 Rows   *2 Columns*

The 'Europe' heading will be set up by:

```
<TH COLSPAN = 2> Europe </TH>
```

The 2 by 2 blank cell at the top left will be set up by:

```
<TH ROWSPAN = 2 COLSPAN = 2>  </TH>
```

The row after this one will only have three entries as the first column will already be occupied. Similarly in the bottom row, the previous row starts with the double-cell heading:

```
<TH ROWSPAN = 2> 14 nights </TH>
```

Look for these, and the other two multi-cell items in the full code for this table.

```
<HTML>
<TITLE> Table with Headings</TITLE>
<BODY BGCOLOR = FFFFFF TEXT = 000000>

<TABLE BORDER = 5 CELLSPACING = 5 CELLPADDING = 5>
<CAPTION>
<H3> Up and Away Holidays </H3>
</CAPTION>
```

```
<TR>
      <TH ROWSPAN = 2 COLSPAN = 2> </TH>
      <TH> US </TH>
      <TH COLSPAN = 2> Europe </TH>
</TR>
<TR>
      <TH> Florida </TH>
      <TH> Malaga </TH>
      <TH> Tuscany </TH>
</TR>
<TR>
      <TH> 7 nights </TH>
      <TH> Full Board </TH>
      <TD> £479 </TD>
      <TD> £399 </TD>
      <TD> £359 </TD>
</TR>
<TR>
      <TH ROWSPAN = 2> 14 nights </TH>
      <TH> Full Board </TH>
      <TD> £629 </TD>
      <TD> £519 </TD>
      <TD> £539 </TD>
</TR>
<TR>
      <TH> Self-Catering </TH>
      <TD> £529 </TD>
      <TD COLSPAN = 2 ALIGN = Center> £419 </TD>
</TR>
</TABLE>
</BODY>
</HTML>
```

Only three items in this following row

Double-depth row heading

Table entries are normally left-aligned

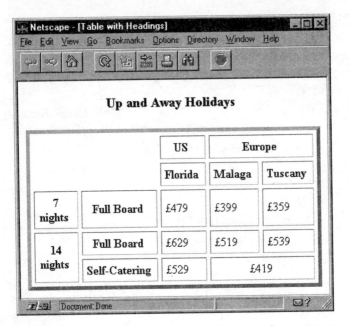

The displayed table, with headings and entries spanning across rows and down columns.

8.7 Alignment

You will have noticed in the last example that an ALIGN option was set for the last <TD...> item. Normally <TH> headings are aligned in the centre of their cells, both vertically and horizontally, and <TD> items are aligned to the left, in the middle of the space. If needed, these can be changed.

These options apply to both <TH> and <TD> tags.

ALIGN = can take the values *Left*, *Center*, or *Right* to set the horizontal alignment.

VALIGN = can take the values Top, Middle or Bottom to set the vertical alignment.

Here's another version of the table, with alignments set for the last row.

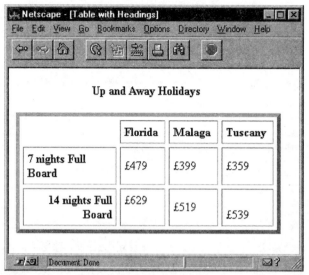

The relevant part of the code reads:

```
<TR>
        <TH ALIGN = Right> 14 nights Full Board</TH>
        <TD VALIGN = Top> £629 </TD>
        <TD VALIGN = Middle> £519 </TD>
        <TD VALIGN = Bottom> £539 </TD>
</TR>
```

VARYING DISPLAYS

Tables adjust to fit the browser window. The row headings in the screenshot above have been wrapped onto two lines. With a wider window they would each have fitted on one line – and the vertical alignment effects would not have been visible in the narrow rows!

—————8.8 Images and links —————

Tables can hold any kind of items – not just text. If you intend exhibiting photographs or other artwork on your home page, it's a good idea to offer your visitors thumbnail previews. The six pictures in the next example occupy just over 20Kb in total as thumbnails – smaller than any individual picture at full size.

Thumbnails can be arranged conveniently in a table. Each can carry a link to a separate page with a full version of the picture. It is then up to your visitors whether or not they take the time to download them.

To set up a thumbnail table, each <TD> entry will need a link to its associated page, the image, and brief descriptive text. They fit together in this pattern:

```
<TD> <A HREF...> <IMG SRC ...> Text </A> </TD>
```

This makes both the picture and the text 'clickable'.

As this is likely to produce a very long line, you will have more readable code if you split it, at a convenient point, into two lines. You can see this in the example below.

```
<HTML>
<TITLE> Thumbnail Table </TITLE>
<TABLE>
<CAPTION>
<H2> Views of the Dribble Valley </H2>
</CAPTION>
    <TR>
      <TD> <A HREF = bar.htm> <IMG SRC = bar.jpg>
      <BR>In the Green Gnome (26Kb)</A> </TD>
      <TD> <A HREF = bridge.htm> <IMG SRC = bridge.jpg>
      <BR>The Dribble bridge (28Kb)</A></TD>
    </TR>
```

Image

Link

Text

Close link

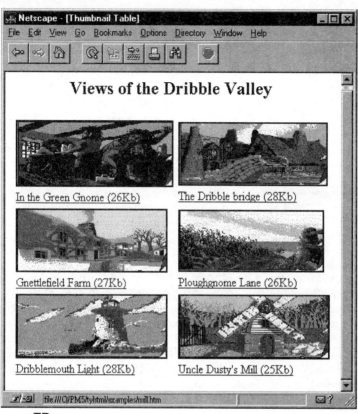

```
    <TR>
        <TD> <A HREF = farm.htm> <IMG SRC = farm.jpg>
        <BR>Gnettlefield Farm (27Kb)</A> </TD>
        <TD> <A HREF = hill.htm> <IMG SRC = hill.jpg>
        <BR>Ploughgnome Lane (26Kb)</A> </TD>
    </TR>
    <TR>
        <TD> <A HREF = light.htm> <IMG SRC = light.jpg>
        <BR>Dribblemouth Light (28Kb)</A> </TD>
```

```
    <TD> <A HREF = mill.htm> <IMG SRC = mill.jpg>
    <BR>Uncle Dusty's Mill (25Kb)</A> </TD>
  </TR>
 </TABLE>
</HTML>
```

—————— **8.9 Tables and layouts** ——————

We have noted that borders can be set to any size. If you drop
the BORDER WIDTH down to 0, the borders disappear but the
table is still there to provide a framework for holding images
and text. We can use this to create newspaper style columns
and other interesting layouts.

The next example has three tables, rather than one. There are
two reasons for this. It allows us to have different numbers of
columns, and different widths, so we can allocate space as needed
for the images and text at each point in the display. It also affects
the way that the page downloads. A table has to be fully
downloaded before it can be displayed – so large tables leave
your visitors waiting for some little time. With several tables,
your visitors can read the first while waiting for the others to
come in.

Each table in this example is only one row deep. The one at the
top has three columns, with an image in the centre. The other
two each have two columns, with images placed in opposite sides.

Here's the source code:

```
<HTML>
<HEAD>
  <TITLE>Tables and layout</TITLE>
</HEAD>
<BODY>
```

```
<TABLE BORDER WIDTH = 0 CELLSPACING = 10
CELLPADDING = 0 COLS = 3>
<TR>
<TD>
<H4>Tables made to order. E-mail for details</H4>
</TD>
<TD>
<H3><IMG SRC = Table1.gif HEIGHT = 38 WIDTH = 200></H3>
</TD>
```

```
<TD><H4>Special summer sale now on!</H4>
</TD>
</TR>
</TABLE>


<TABLE CELLSPACING = 0 CELLPADDING = 0 COLS = 2>
<TR>
<TD WIDTH = "25%"><IMG SRC = Table2.gif HEIGHT = 108
WIDTH = 168></TD>
<TD>
<H2>The King Arthur</H2>
<H3>A round table for nights of dining pleasure</H3>
</TD>
</TR>
</TABLE>


<TABLE CELLSPACING = 0 CELLPADDING = 0 COLS = 2>
<TR>
<TD>
<H2>The Great Hall</H2>
This refectory table is ideal for the larger family. Available in
10', 14' and 18' length</TD>
<TD WIDTH = "80%"><IMG SRC = Table3.gif HEIGHT = 121
WIDTH = 241></TD>
</TR>
</TABLE>
</BODY>
</HTML>
```

8.10 Summary

- Tables can be used to display text items, images or links.

- Tables are tag-intensive. Every data item must be enclosed in a pair of <TD> tags; every heading in <TH> tags; every row in <TR> tags.

- Borders can be added, and the thickness and spacing of their lines set by options.

- A caption can be placed above or below a table.

- Headings and data items can be spread across several columns, or down several rows if necessary.

- The text or image in a data cell or heading can be aligned vertically and horizontally.

- Tables are a good way of displaying thumbnail images if you are running an on-line 'gallery'.

- Tables allow you to lay out blocks of text alongside images – and if you set the BORDER WIDTH to 0, the frame will become invisible.

9

FRAMES

Netscape 2.0

9.1 Aims of this chapter

If you are using Netscape or Internet Explorer 3.0 or later, you will no doubt have seen other people's frame-based Web pages, and probably thought to yourself that they looked good, but complicated to do.

Have no fear! Frames are actually quite easy to implement. In this chapter we will work through the stages of setting up frames and linking documents into them.

9.2 The frame concept

With frames, you have two distinct types of document:

- *Layout documents* create the frames. They normally carry no displayed content whatsoever – their function is purely to divide the window up into areas.

● *Content documents* go into the frames. They are identical
to normal pages, though you may need to adjust their links
if the pages are to call each other up within the frame
window. While you experimenting, you can use any of your
existing pages as contents documents, without alteration.
Later, you might want to edit and redesign them so that
they work better in the new environment.

Fitting them together

A layout document can divide a window into any number of
frames, either vertically or horizontally – but not both. However,
a frame can hold another layout document, which can subdivide
either vertically or horizontally. The nesting of frames within
frames can go on *ad infinitum*, but in practice you wouldn't want
to use more than two or three layout documents or a total of
more than half a dozen content frames in one design – it would
just be too confusing for both you and your visitors.

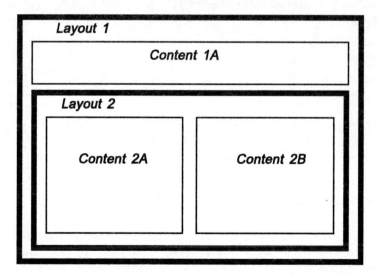

In the diagram, **Layout 1** contains two frames:

> **Content 1**
>
> **Layout 2**   containing two frames
>
> > **Content 2A**
> >
> > **Content 2B**

What's in the Content documents is irrelevant at this stage – though crucial when you do it for real. A good way to use your frames is to have one that displays your logo, title or other identifier – this would stay on show permanently. A second frame will hold an index or contents list which allows your visitors to navigate through the set of pages that are displayed in the third frame. A large or complex site might have several contents lists which could be switched into the second frame to give access to different sets of pages.

The frame structure does not have to remain fixed. You can load a new layout document into a frame, or into the whole window, to give a different structure – and to link to new sets of contents documents.

————9.3 Layout documents————

There are three tags which apply only to layout documents – in fact, a layout document would normally only use these three, apart from <HTML> and <TITLE>.

<FRAMESET ROWS / COLS = Value, Value>

This defines the division of the window into frames. It can take either the ROWS or the COLS option – but not both – depending upon which way you want to divide. There is a *Value* for every division.

The Values can be given in three ways, and you would normally use two of these when defining the divisions:

Fixed   sets the width or depth of a frame in pixels:

           ROWS = 150,...

Percent   sets the width or depth as a percentage of the browser window size:

           COLS = 25%, ...

Relative   sets the width or depth as a fraction of the remaining area. The symbol '*' used by itself simply means all the rest of the space:

           ROWS = 200,*

           sets up two frames, the first 200 pixels deep, the second taking up whatever space is left below.

* can also mean 'fraction', when used with a number.

    COLS = *, 3*

This says, 'divide the window into two columns, with the second column being 3 times as wide as the first'. It has the same effect as ...

    COLS = 25%, 75%

... but is quicker to write.

* is useful where you have a mix of fixed and percentage sizes:

    ROWS = 100, 25%, *

This creates three horizontal frames. The top one is 100 pixels deep, the second is 25% of the window height, and the third is whatever space is left.

</FRAMESET>

This closes the frame definition part. Between <FRAMESET...> and </FRAMESET> you define the contents of the frames using <FRAME ...>

<FRAME SRC = ... >

This is where you specify the document to be placed into the frame. Assuming that the document is another file in the same directory as the layout document, the tag might read:

```
<FRAME SRC = banner.htm>
```

If the frame is to be used to display pages,which will be selected from a contents list in another frame, it should have a name:

```
<FRAME SRC = toppage.htm NAME = showplace>
```

This frame will display the *toppage.htm* file when it first opens, then be used to display other pages that will be directed into it from elsewhere. We'll come back to this in section 9.4.

The tag also takes some options to define the nature of the frame.

```
NORESIZE
```

Fixes the size of the frame.

```
SCROLLING = Yes/No/Auto
```

Forces scrollbars to be on (Yes), off (No), or leave it to the system to switch them on and off as necessary(Auto).

Let's put these together. The following code will only work properly if you have files called *banner.htm* and *inframe.htm*. Without them, you will get messages complaining abou the missing files, but the frame structure will still be visible.

Fixed size frame at the top

```
<HTML>
<FRAMESET ROWS = 100,*>
  <FRAME SRC = banner.htm NORESIZE SCROLLING = No>
  <FRAME SRC = inframe.htm SCROLLING = Auto>
</FRAMESET>
</HTML>
```

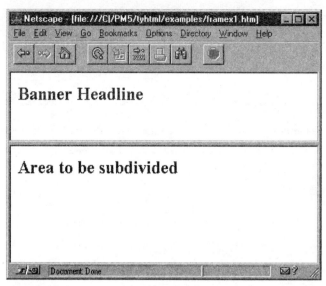

In this example, the banner.htm *and* inframe.htm *files held simple headings, just so that something was visible.*

If you wanted to keep things simple, you could stop at a two-frame display, putting a title graphic or text in the banner frame and your home page document in the main frame. Open the layout file in Netscape, both contents documents should load in, and any pages linked from your top page should display in the main frame, when their links are activated.

But let's press on to create a two-layout, three-frame display. You need this second layout file, to be saved as *inframe.htm*.

```
<HTML>                         ———— The left frame is narrow
<FRAMESET COLS = 30%,*>
  <FRAME SRC = navigate.htm>
  <FRAME SRC = content.htm NAME = contents>
</FRAMESET>
</HTML>
```

Here is the output, with temporary text in the *navigate.htm* and *content.htm* files. In the working version, *navigate.htm* would hold a set of links to act as an index to the pages, and *content.htm* would be the first page of the display.

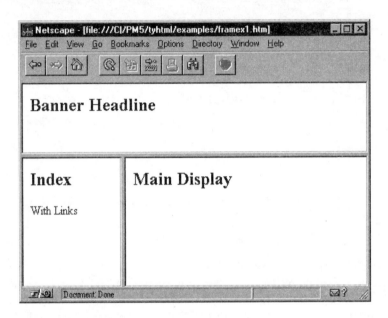

<NOFRAMES>

Frames are only visible to those visitors running Netscape 2.0 – what about the rest? The answer lies in the <NOFRAMES> pair of tags. These can be used, inside the <FRAMESET ...> tags, to enclose text, links and other material that will be visible on browsers that cannot handle frames. (The enclosed code is ignored by Netscape 2.0.)

We can then set up a <NOFRAMES> section that gives a minimal welcome message and directs our visitors to the home page that would otherwise be reached through a link in the frames.

```
<HTML>

<FRAMESET ROWS = 100,*>

   <NOFRAMES>
           This page uses Netscape 2.0 frames. <BR>
           Click <A HREF = index.htm> here </A> for the
           no-frame version.
   </NOFRAMES>
... other frame stuff ...
</FRAMESET>

</HTML>
```

Viewed in Explorer, the frame page now looks like this:

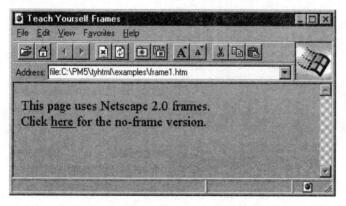

FRAMES AND NOFRAMES

It can be tricky getting a site to look equally good in frame
and no-frame versions. Stick to a fairly simple structure and
you should be OK. In the frames, have an index frame to
link to your other display pages, but put links in these so that
it is possible to navigate through the pages without using
the index frame. The links will be redundant in the frame
version, but make the site workable to other people.

—————— 9.4 Links and targets ——————

When you create a link to a page from a simple page, there is no question as to where the new page is displayed – it replaces the calling one. When you have frames, there is a question of where to display the linked page. The answer is supplied through a new option in the <A HREF ...> tag.

<A HREF = "url" TARGET = ...>

Using frames, you have five alternative targets – places in which a linked page can be displayed.

TARGET =

framename displays in the frame identified as framename in its <FRAME SRC = ... NAME = framename> tag

_self displays in the current frame. If you omit the TARGET phrase, it has the same effect.

_parent replaces the layout document containing the linking frame, with the new page – which may well be a new layout document, giving a new structure.

_top replaces the top level layout document, i.e. the whole window, with the new page.

_blank opens a new copy of the browser and displays the page in there. You can have as many Netscape windows running at once as you like!

For example:

    <A HREF = myclub.htm TARGET = mainframe>

This displays the *myclub* page in the *mainframe* frame.

    <A HREF = newframe.htm TARGET = _parent>

Replaces the current layout document with the *newframe* one.

—— 9.5 The framed home page ——

If you have followed the examples so far, you should now have the skeleton of a three-frame window. All it needs is some flesh.

Design your own Home Page logo or graphic title, or create a strong, coloured text heading, to fit into the top frame. Save it as *banner.htm*. (If you have already got something suitable, change the SRC reference in the top level layout document.) The one used in the next screenshots looks like this:

```
<HTML>
<BODY BGCOLOR = FFFFFF>
<IMG SRC = tylogo.gif WIDTH = 100%>
</BODY>
</HTML>                              Set it to fill the window
```

The index frame

The index, or contents list, frame – called *navigate.htm* in the earlier example – holds links to all the pages that you want to display. A <UL> list offers a neat way of presenting them.

At the simplest you can set the *contents* frame as the TARGET for them all, but experiment with the alternatives.

● If you use **TARGET = _self** (or miss out the TARGET phrase), the incoming document will overwrite your index. This will need a return link of the type:

   <A HREF = navigate.htm> Return to the Index </A>

● If you use **TARGET = _top** or **TARGET = _parent**, the incoming document will replace a layout document. This will also need a return link:

   <A HREF = topframe.htm> Return to the Home Page </A>

The page in the screenshot opposite uses this Index document. (I've pruned some of the links to save space and because they don't show anything new.)

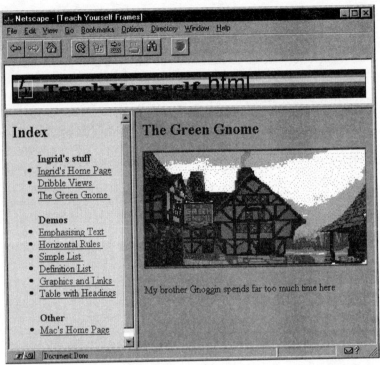

At this point, one of the Ingrid links has been activated, displaying the page in the contents frame.

```
<HTML>
<H2> Index </H2>
<UL>
<B>Ingrid's stuff</B>
<LI><A HREF = ingrid.htm TARGET = contents>
Ingrid's Home Page</A>
<LI><A HREF = views.htm TARGET = _blank>
Dribble Views </A>
<LI><A HREF = ggnome.htm TARGET = contents>
The Green Gnome </A>
<P>
```

```
<B>Demos</B>
<LI><A HREF = emphasis.htm TARGET = contents>
Emphasising Text </A>
```

```
<LI><A HREF = lines.htm TARGET = contents> Horizontal
Rules </A>
```

```
<LI><A HREF = list1.htm TARGET = contents> Simple List </A>
```

```
<LI><A HREF = deflist.htm TARGET = contents> Definition
List </A>
```

```
<LI><A HREF = clee.htm TARGET = contents> Graphics and
Links </A>
```

```
<LI><A HREF = table4.htm TARGET = contents> Table with
Headings </A>
```

```
<P> <B> Other </B>
<LI><A HREF = machome.htm TARGET = _top>
Mac's Home Page</A>
</UL>
</HTML>
```

Contents pages

Any of your existing HTML documents can be displayed in the *contents* frame, or wherever you choose to target them. If you have designed them to work in windows of any size, then the fact that they are displayed in a frame, not the full screen, should not matter.

As noted already, you may need to do a little editing:

● Where a page replaces the inner or the top layout document, you must link back to it to restore the original frame structure.

● If you want the site to be viewable in browsers other than Netscape 2.0, you must provide links between the pages, so that visitors can still navigate between them.

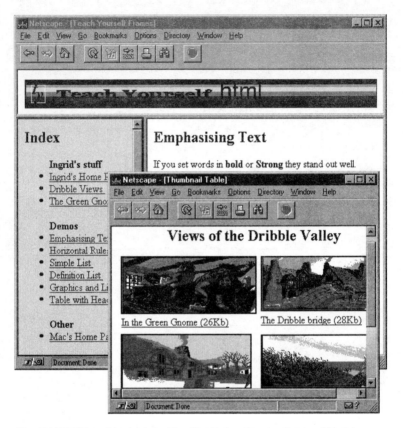

The TARGET = _blank option for the Green Gnome has opened a new browser window. Other links could be run from here if wanted.

● If you are including links to other people's pages, these will not have links back to you (unless you have arranged it with them). These must be targeted into your contents area or a new blank window, so that your index frame remains visible, if you want your visitors to be able to get back to you.

------------------ **9.6 Summary** ------------------

- Frame displays are much easier to set up that you might think at first sight.

- With frames, the structure is created in layout documents; the display in contents documents.

- The <FRAMESET> tag defines the number and size of the divisions.

- The <FRAME> tag specifies the (layout or contents) document to use when the frame is first opened.

- Frames should be given NAMEs, if they are to be the TARGET for an incoming page.

- In a frame display, you normally use one frame to hold an index, for your visitors to navigate through your pages.

IMAGE MAPS AND FRAMES

There is another example of frames – this time using an image map as an index – at the end of the next chapter.

10

IMAGE MAPS

10.1 Aims of this chapter

A good image map can give a slick professional appearance to your home page – and a bad one can really put visitors off! The difference is all in the design, and I can't help much there. What I can do in this chapter is look at the practical aspects of producing an image map. There are two ways of going about it. The easy way is to get a bit of software to do the job for you; the hard way is to do it all yourself – though even that is not so hard.

CLIENT SIDE IMAGE MAPS

If you have version 2 or later of Netscape or Internet Explorer, you can run a *client side* map – i.e. the whole thing can be handled from your home page. With earlier browsers you can only use *server side* maps, and for these you need an obliging remote host to do the processing for you. We are only concerned here with client side maps.

10.2 Drawing the map

There aren't any rules on this. The graphic can be a photograph, scanned image or painted picture; it can be an integrated design or a collection of small images on a common background; plain or fancy text can be added if desired. All that is essential is that you keep its purpose in mind, and work towards that. Your visitors should be able to identify easily where they should click and what will happen when they click there.

If you have MapEdit, or similar Image Map software, the only other thing you need to do after creating the image is convert it into a GIF or JPG file. If you are doing it all yourself, go over the image and note the co-ordinates of the top left and bottom right corners of the areas that hold each clickable part.

The Status line shows us that the top left of the Green Gnome picture is at 187, 172. Record these co-ordinates if you are taking the DIY route.

————— 10.3 The map page —————

An image map can sit at the top of a much longer home page, or it can fit into a frame, or it can form a home page by itself. However you do it, your page should also include plain text links to the same places, so that visitors can still get there, even if they choose not to load the image.

In the example page here, I have used the same background colour – black – for the page, as for the image. This helps to give a uniform appearance to the page, though once the image map has been set up properly, it will be distinguished from the background by an outline in the text colour. Note that the LINK and VLINK colours have had to be changed so that the links are visible.

The other minor point worth noting here is the way that the links have been separated. I have put * – any character would have done – between each pair so that they do not form a continuous line of text.

```
<HTML>
<TITLE> Image Map </TITLE>
<BODY BGCOLOR = 000000 TEXT = FFFFFF LINK =
FFFF00 VLINK = 00FFFF>
<IMG SRC = imagemap.gif>        These 4 pages will be
<P>                             linked from the image map
<A HREF = machome.htm>Mac </A> *
<A HREF = tylogo.htm>Teach Yourself </A> *
<A HREF = ingrid.htm>Ingrid's Home Page </A> *
<A HREF = soton.htm> What's on in Soton </A>
</BODY>
</HTML>
```

Save the file at this stage and check its appearance in your browser. When you are happy with the design, move on.

The basic HTML document, with its image, before mapping.

——— 10.4 Linking code ———

The first job is to define which graphic is to be the image map. The graphic needs a name by which it will be known inside the document. It may as well be based on the filename, but could be anything – though it must be a single word and start with #.

Inside the <IMG SRC ...> tag, you add the option USEMAP = giving the image map's name.

```
<IMG SRC = mymap.gif  USEMAP = #mymap>
```

This name is picked up again at the start of the mapping section. This is marked by the <MAP NAME = ...> tag.

```
<MAP NAME = mymap>
```

Note that the # is omitted here. The use of # in map names reflects its use in the names of jump points (see Chapter 4).

Inside the <MAP ...> section, you define each area of the map which is to carry a link. The definitions look like this:

```
<AREA SHAPE = "rect" COORDS = "15,120,115,240" HREF
= "machome.htm">
```

Let's break that line down into its parts:

<AREA	marks the start of the tag;
SHAPE =	either *rect*, *circle*, *polygon* or *default*
COORDS =	are the co-ordinates that define the shape.
HREF = ...>	the URL of the page to be linked to the area.

Co-ordinates

The pattern of co-ordinates depends upon the shape. Working from the shapes in the diagram below:

for *rect*, give the top left and bottom right corners; e.g.

COORDS = 25, 25, 100, 75

for *circle* give the centre, followed by the radius; e.g.

COORDS = 200, 50, 25

for *polygon*, give the x,y co-ordinates of each point: e.g.

COORDS = 100, 100, 200, 100, 150, 50, 100, 100

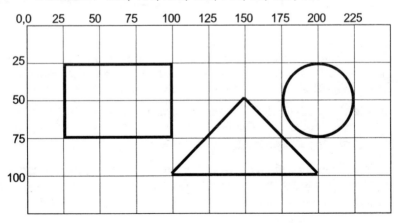

The background of the image – everything not enclosed by a shape – can be refered to as *default*. You can also link a page to here, or if you do not want this to be 'clickable', set it to NOHREF.

```
<AREA SHAPE = "default" NOHREF>
```

If you haven't worked out the co-ordinates of the clickable areas on your map, load the graphic back into Paint or PaintShop Pro and read the co-ordinates off the Status line as you point to the corners of the areas.

Mark the end of the <MAP ...> section with the tag </MAP>.

The example given here works for my image map only.

```
<HTML>
<TITLE> Image Map </TITLE>
<BODY BGCOLOR = "000000" TEXT = "FFFFFF" LINK =
"FFFF00" VLINK = "00FFFF">
<IMG SRC = "imagemap.gif" USEMAP = "#imagemap"> <P>
<A HREF = "machome.htm">Mac </A> *
<A HREF = "tylogo.htm">Teach Yourself </A> *
<A HREF = "ingrid.htm">Ingrid's Home Page </A> *
<A HREF = "soton.htm"> What's on in Soton </A>
<MAP NAME = "imagemap">
<AREA SHAPE = "rect" COORDS = "15,120,115,240" HREF
= "machome.htm">
<AREA SHAPE = "rect" COORDS = "210,20,280,90" HREF =
"tylogo.htm">
<AREA SHAPE = "rect" COORDS = "190,170,330,250" HREF
= "ingrid.htm">
<AREA SHAPE = "circle" COORDS = "175,160,25" HREF =
"soton.htm">
<AREA SHAPE = "default" NOHREF>
</MAP>
</BODY>
</HTML>
```

—————— 10.5 MapEdit ——————

If that last section has left you feeling that there ought to be an easier way to set up image maps, then this section is for you. MapEdit, from Boutell Inc, is a simple and effective solution. Get an evaluation copy from them at:

http://www.boutell.com/index.html

MapEdit is available for Windows 3.1 or 95, Mac, Unix and other major systems. Select the one you need and download it from their home page. It comes in as a smallish ZIP file – the Windows 95 version was just over 160Kb – which should be unZIPped into a suitable directory.

To use MapEdit, first prepare your map image and place it in an HTML document – any required text or text links can also be added at this stage. Save the document and run MapEdit.

Give the **File|Open** command, and at the **Open/Create Map** dialog box, **Browse** for the HTML file containing your map.

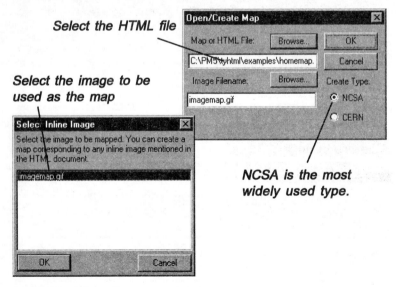

Select the HTML file

Select the image to be used as the map

NCSA is the most widely used type.

MapEdit will scan the file and pick up any image references. You will then be asked which one to map. (The document could have any number of images in it – for that matter, you could set up several image maps on different images in one document.)

Once the image is loaded in, you can start to create clickable areas on it. Select your shape, then click the top left and bottom right corners for a rectangle, the centre and edge for a circle, or a sequence of points for a polygon. MapEdit then asks for the URL to be linked to that area. ALT text, for visitors who don't load graphics, can be defined at this stage, and if you are working in frames, you can set the TARGET for the linked page to be displayed in.

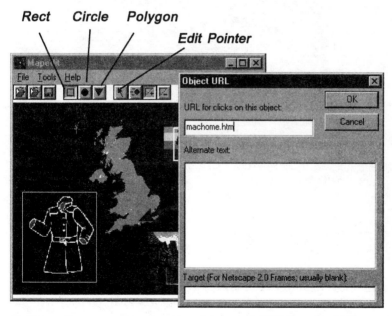

If afterwards you need to change a shape, or its URL, use the Edit Pointer to select the area then make your alterations.

As you add areas, their outlines remain visible – these will not be displayed in the working map. Shapes can overlap, but note that a click in the overlap area will select the first area to have been defined.

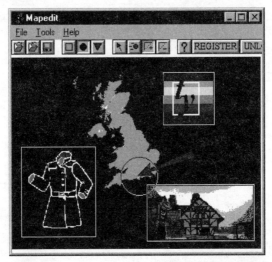

When you have finished, save the file. If you then open it in your word-processor, you will see that MapEdit has written the code for you. If necessary, you can make further adjustments or addition 'by hand'.

—— 10.6 Image maps in frames ——

This next example is mainly here to show how image maps can be used to navigate within frames, but it is also good opportunity to revisit the frame concept.

The aim is to produce a screen that carries a logo, a title bar and an image map, in three frames around a main display area. We start with a sketch, to work out the structure of frames.

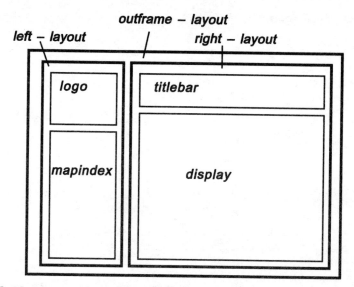

The logo area is approximately 200 x 200 pixels. The titlebar can be flexible in size, but should occupy about 15% of the height. That leads us to these layout documents:

outframe.htm

```
<HTML>
<TITLE>cOn-Line </TITLE>          width of logo frame
<FRAMESET COLS = 200,*>
  <FRAME SRC = left.htm NORESIZE SCROLLING = Yes>
  <FRAME SRC = right.htm SCROLLING = Auto>
</FRAMESET>
</HTML>
```

left.htm

```
                                  height of logo frame
<HTML>
<FRAMESET ROWS = 200,*>
  <FRAME SRC = logo.htm NORESIZE SCROLLING = No>
  <FRAME SRC = mapindex.htm SCROLLING = Auto>
```

```
</FRAMESET>
</HTML>
```

right.htm

```
<HTML>
<FRAMESET ROWS = 15%,*>
 <FRAME SRC = titlebar.htm NORESIZE SCROLLING = No>
 <FRAME SRC = display.htm NAME = display>
</FRAMESET>
</HTML>
```

The contents of the logo, titlebar and display documents are irrelevant – you can see what I have used in the illustration on the next page. My example firm, cOn-line, is one of those who aim to make money from the incredulous. You can probably guess that from the image map.

The index image map, seen here through MapEdit so that the clickable areas are highlighted, links to three documents that will be targeted at the display window. Note that the target is set in the bottom slot of the **Object URL** dialog box.

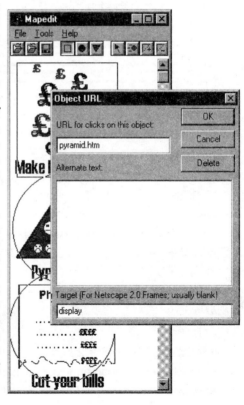

There is one more image map in this page – the logo in the top left has been mapped so that if it is clicked, the welcome document is reloaded into the *display* frame. It is useful to have a means of restoring a display if your visitors could wander off down routes that do not lead back directly. If incoming documents overwrite the whole of the right layout document, then the restore link should be targeted to that whole area.

```
<HTML>
<IMG SRC = "conlogo.gif" USEMAP = "#conlogo">
<MAP NAME = "conlogo">
<AREA SHAPE = "rect" COORDS = "1,1,150,150" HREF =
"display.htm" TARGET = display>
<AREA SHAPE = "default" NOHREF>
</MAP>
</HTML>
```

10.7 Summary

- Any graphic can be used as an image map, though it must be in GIF or JPG format, and should be easily understood by your visitors.

- An image map can sit anywhere in a page. You can have several image maps in the same document, if required.

- You should provide text link alternatives to the map, for those visitors that cannot or do not want to download graphics.

- Image maps are defined with the <MAP NAME = ...> tag.

- Each clickable area must be set up with a <AREA...> tag, giving the co-ordinates to define its outline.

- The MapEdit program, from Boutell Inc, offers an easy way to create image maps.

- Image maps can be a good way to navigate through a frame display.

11

ACTIVE PAGES

11.1 Aims of this chapter

In this chapter we will look at some of the ways in which you can add activity and interactivity to your pages – and without getting too technical! Animated GIFs are perhaps the easiest way to liven up a static page, and background music can be added without too much effort. For interactivity, you must turn to a programming language – JavaScript, Java or ActiveX. If you have the time, you could learn one of these and write your own code from scratch. The quick alternative is to search the Internet for ready-made examples and applets, and adapt them to suit your site. We will look briefly at the two most commonly used languages, JavaScript and Java.

11.2 Animated GIFs

An animated GIF is a set of GIF images, which are stored as one file, and displayed in succession at timed intervals. Any modern browser can display them, and any decent graphics

software can be used to create the set of images, but you will
need special software to turn them into an animation.

The images

These should be all the same size and saved in the standard
GIF format. How many you will need depends on the amount of
change you want to make, and the degree of smoothness you
want between the frames. Start with a minimal set – the initial
image, the end image and a couple of the stages in between.
You can always add extra 'tween' images later.

Keep downloading times in mind! The animation file will be
fractionally smaller than the sum of the individual files – half a
dozen 5Kb GIFs (about 100 pixels square) will produce an
animation of around 25Kb, which will download in about 10
seconds. With larger animations, you might want to let your
visitors know what's coming and that it is worth waiting for!

Microsoft GIF Animator

One of the best (free) GIF animation programs around is
Microsoft GIF Animator, which is currently supplied as part of
the ImageComposer suite. This can be downloaded from
Microsoft's home site, **http://www.microsoft.com**. It's about
1.5Mb (10 to 20 minutes download time) and you get a fully-
featured graphics package along with your GIF animator!

Here's how to create an animated GIF.

1 Click the ![icon] **Open** button and select the first image.
2 Click the ![icon] **Insert** button and select the next image. It
   will be inserted above the first – use ![icon] to move it down.
3 Insert and move the rest in the same way.
4 Switch to the **Animation** tab, turn on **Looping** and set
   the **Repeat Count** or turn on **Repeat Forever**.

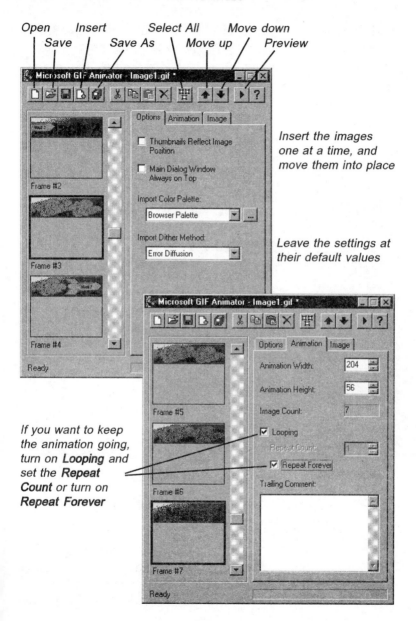

Open / Insert / Select All / Move down
Save / Save As / Move up / Preview

Insert the images one at a time, and move them into place

Leave the settings at their default values

*If you want to keep the animation going, turn on **Looping** and set the **Repeat Count** or turn on **Repeat Forever***

5 Before you do anything else, save the file – there is a bug which can cause the program to crash at the next stage! Click the 🗗 **Save As** button and give the file a name.

6 Switch to the **Image** tab.

7 If you want to set the same delay for all (or most) images, click the 🔣 **Select All** button, then set the **Duration**.

8 Otherwise, select each image in turn and set its **Duration**.

9 Click the ▶ **Preview** button and see how it looks. If necessary, close the Preview window and and adjust the Durations to you get the effect you want.

10 Click the 🖫 **Save** button to save your changes.

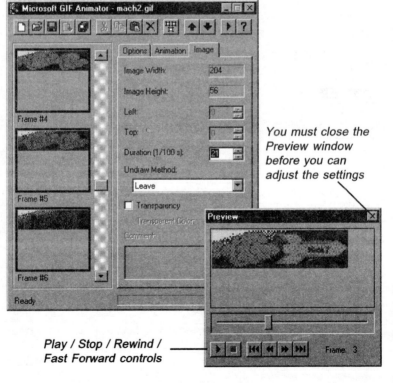

You must close the Preview window before you can adjust the settings

Play / Stop / Rewind / Fast Forward controls

11.3 JavaScript

JavaScript is one of the easiest programming languages to learn – largely because you do not have to write complete programs to produce results! JavaScript code is written into the HTML documents, and is interpreted and executed by the browser – but note that it can only be handled by Netscape 2.0 or newer, or Internet Explorer 4.0 Earlier Explorers will not do.

The code may consist of a single instruction, attached to a button on a form, and activated by a click. For example:

```
<INPUT TYPE = button VALUE = "Click me"
   onClick = "alert('Hello visitor')">
```

When the button is clicked, the **onClick** event is picked up by Netscape, which then runs the attached code. This opens an alert message box, carrying the greeting. The quotes in that line are crucial. The JavaScript code is enclosed in double quotes; the text of the message is enclosed in single quotes.

This idea is taken a little further in the next example, where the message box carries a greeting to the visitor. The code reads:

```
onClick = "alert('Hello ' + form.user.value)"
```

This is used with an text box named 'user'. The code reads the contents of that box and adds it to the 'Hello' to form a greeting.

Simple responses to button clicks are easily done in JavaScript

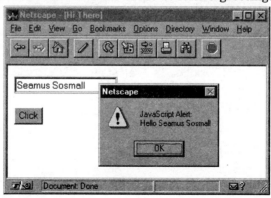

Here's the complete code:

```
<HTML>
<BODY>
<FORM>
<INPUT TYPE = text NAME = user VALUE = "Name please">
<P><INPUT TYPE = button VALUE = "Click"
    onClick = "alert('Hello ' + form1.user.value)">
</FORM>
</BODY>
</HTML>
```

If you want to display a message in the Status line, you can do this from JavaScript. The expression takes the format:

```
self.status = "message"
```

self refers to the current window.

The code could be activated from a button click, or when the page is loaded. In the latter case, we attach to the **onLoad** event, which fits into the BODY tag. This gives us the line:

```
<BODY onLoad = "self.status = 'Welcome to my page' ">
```

Again, notice those quotes – double round the whole lot; single quotes around text within the code.

Here's a working example, with a message appearing when the page loads, and a new one when the user clicks the button.

```
<HTML>
<BODY onLoad = "self.status = 'Welcome to my page' ">
<FORM>
<INPUT TYPE = button VALUE = "Going?"
    onClick = "self.status = 'Thanks for dropping by' ">
</FORM>
</BODY>
</HTML>
```

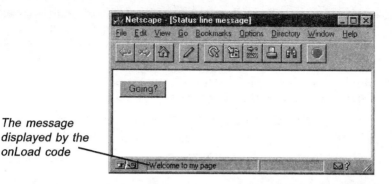

The message displayed by the onLoad code

These little examples demonstrate what you can do with just a couple of lines of JavaScript. There are plenty of bigger examples around on the Internet – there are a few in my JavaScript Sampler at **http://www.tcp.co.uk/~macbride**.

If you want to find more, go to **Yahoo** and look in the **Computers and Internet>Programming Languages>JavaScript** section.

11.4 Java applets

Java applets are self-contained programs that run within Web pages. They are pulled into the page through the <APPLET> tag which specifies the applet code and sets the size of the display area. To cater for those users who cannot, or do not want to, view applets, alternative text or an image can be included. This example runs the *piano* applet in a 500 x 400 box, or displays the message if the browser cannot handle Java.

```
<APPLET CODE = "piano.class" WIDTH = 500 HEIGHT = 400>
    If you had Java you could play my piano!
</APPLET>
```

It is very satisfying to write your own applets, but learning Java properly is a major undertaking. You may prefer to make use of other people's efforts. The Internet has plenty of ready-written applets which you can adapt to suit your pages – though these tend to carry (prominent and undeletable) adverts for the original author's site.

Applets can be customised through the use of *parameters*. Values can be passed from HTML to the applet through <PARAM> tags.

```
<APPLET CODE = banner.class WIDTH = 500 HEIGHT = 200>
<PARAM NAME = message VALUE = "Welcome to my page">
<IMG SRC = welcome.gif ALT = "This page is better with Java">
</APPLET>
```

This applet has two parameters that let you set the message to be displayed. Notice how it caters for browsers that do not support Java – it will display an image, or text, if images are turned off. Ready-made applets that use parameters will also have the relevant HTML code for downloading. All you will need to do is change the text or numbers in the VALUE expressions.

TEACH YOURSELF JAVA

If you want to learn Java, try Chris Wright's *Teach Yourself Java*, available where you bought this book

---

11.5 Summary

- Animated GIFs catch the eye and are easily produced with software such as Microsoft's GIF Animator.

- JavaScript is not difficult to learn, and even small amounts of code can help to make a page more interactive.

- Java applets can be embedded in HTML pages. You can find ready-made ones on the Internet.

12

HTML EDITORS

12.1 Aims of this chapter

Writing your own HTML code directly gives you far greater
control over the appearance of the document, and – as I hope
you have seen – is not difficult. However, you may find it worth
while experimenting with some of the many HTML editors now
available, to see whether they will do what you want to do, and
whether they will do it more quickly or simply. In this chapter,
we will have a look at some of these editors, to see the kind of
things they have to offer and what limitations they impose.

12.2 Home Page Wizard

This is the software that CompuServe supplies to its members
to create their pages for the Web. It is very easy to use – you
could knock up an 'Hello I'm here' Web page in a matter of
minutes – but it does have its limitations.

When you start the Wizard, it runs you through a set of panels to collect your initial preferences for the page and some personal details. These are incorporated into the text of the page – you can see an example above.

Text, graphics and links are all treated as separate items – you cannot embed a link or a graphic inside a paragraph of text. Text and all other items are added to the page through icons and dialog boxes. These are pretty well idiot-proof. The boxes have separate panels for the text, filename or other specification, and for the style options. These are restricted. You can, for instance, set body text items as bulleted, pre-formatted or centred. There are no size, colour, bold, italic or similar

CompuServe's Home Page Wizard. Most of the icons lead to dialog boxes where you enter details and set style options.

formatting options. Lines, on the other hand, are handled well – the full range of size, width and shade options are available.

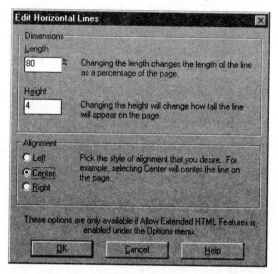

The system is designed around projects – multi-page displays, and provides easy means of linking between pages. The ease of movement, and the ease with which new pages can be created, offset some of the limitations of Home Page Wizard. A large set of simply designed pages can be as effective as one or two more complex ones. All pages must be created within the Wizard – you cannot pull in ones designed elsewhere; nor can you edit the pages to add your own bells and whistles, as they are saved in a special non-text format.

When you have completed your pages, you can upload them with a simple click of the Publish icon. (Well, that's the theory. CompuServe's Web site is so busy so much of the time it can be very difficult to get a working connection long enough to upload your project.)

As we saw in Chapter 5, the publishing wizard can be used independently to upload hand-written pages.

——————— 12.3 Netscape's Editor ———————

Netscape first packaged an editor in the Gold edition of 2.0. The editor is still there, virtually unchanged, as Composer in the Communicator set.

The editor does have its limitations – you cannot set up forms or create frames with it – but it is excellent for formatting text, inserting links, targets and images. It also makes very light work of creating tables.

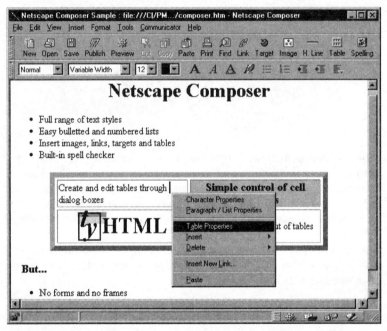

There is a well-organised and comprehensive menu command system, but you may well find that you rarely use it. The very full set of toolbar icons and drop-down lists give access to all the commands and features that are regularly used. Right-clicking on an element or selected text opens a context menu containing a short set of commands relevant to the situation.

The Formatting toolbar contains icons and drop-down lists to handle all aspects of text layout – style, size, colour, emphasis and alignment. Formats can be applied at the start of a new paragraph, or to existing text. Style (Normal, Heading 1, etc.) and alignment options apply to the whole paragraph containing the cursor. Font, size, colour and emphasis options apply only to selected text or to new text.

The toolbar makes it far easier to create fancy text effects, like the roller coaster back in section 2.6!

Clicking on the **Link**, **Target**, **Image** or **Table** icons opens a dialog box for inserting and formatting the element. The **Image Properties** dialog box, shows the level of control that the Netscape Editor gives you over these elements.

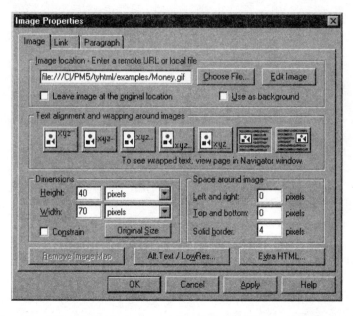

The properties dialog boxes can also be called up by right-clicking on an existing image, link or table.

If you like, you can just do the bare minimum – here you only need to choose the image file – but you can also set the size, alignment, colour, and other aspects, as appropriate.

Notice that the **Image Properties** dialog box has more than one panel. The image may also carry a **Link**, which can be set from here; the **Paragraph** panel is mainly used for setting the alignment across the page, though if the image was embedded in text, its style could be set here.

BMPs to JPGs

One very neat feature of Composer – not present in the earlier Editor – is automatic conversion of bitmap images to JPG format. This allows you to create your images in Paint and take them straight into a page, without having to use special graphics software.

Tables

As you will have gathered from Chapter 8, tables are dreadfully fiddly things to set up, so anything that simplifies the process is to be welcomed. Netscape's Editor certainly does.

Give the **Insert – Table** command, or click the **Table** tool and the **New Table** dialog box opens. Here you can set the basic layout, size, Border and Cell options, and its background colour. It takes only a few seconds, and you have saved yourself the trouble of typing in a whole raft of <TABLE SIZE = ...>, <TR> and <TD> tags!

The **Table Properties** dialog box can be opened later to insert or delete rows and columns, adjust any of the settings, or fine-tune the layout. The Row panel lets you set the alignment and colour options for individual rows. The Cell panel gives you control over the appearance of selected cells – you can set a cell to span several rows or columns from here.

A minute's work on here will save an awful lot of typing!

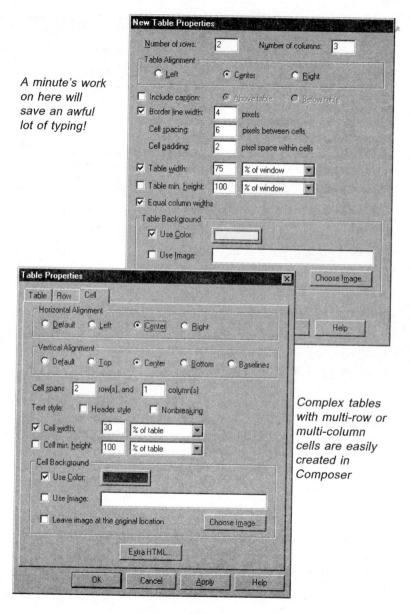

Complex tables with multi-row or multi-column cells are easily created in Composer

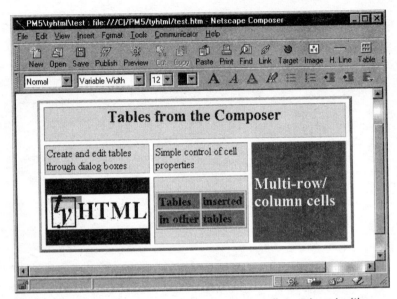

This shows some of the effects that can be easily produced with Composer – cells spanning several columns or rows, coloured backgrounds, inserted images and even a table inserted into a cell.

Forms and frames

If you want to set up a framed system, or a feedback form, you will hit up against the limitations of the Netscape Editor/Composer – it cannot handle these tags. You can link in NotePad or WordPad and use this to edit the source code, though when you get back to Composer, you will see ⟨⟨//⟩ wherever it meets tags it cannot understand. The only way to tell if they are working properly is to hit the Preview button and have a look at the page in Navigator.

Despite the limitations, I find that the combination of Composer and NotePad is a convenient way to produce single pages and smaller multi-page systems. It's only when you turn to large, complex sites that you need much more power.

————12.4 HTML from Word————

If you have Word 97, you can use it to create HTML documents. Start from a Web page template – or better still from the Web Page Wizard.

The Wizard offers ten ready designed pages to meet a range of common situations. Here, for example is the Registration Form. The basic form is set up, with several blank options and text boxes, plus headings and labels. You have a choice of styles, determining its fonts, layout and background – and the same style can be applied to different pages, so you can have a consistent appearance to a multi-page site.

The Registration Form, in Festive style, after some editing. For some strange reason, you cannot edit the drop-down lists within Word. Opening the file in WordPad seems to be about the only way to get at the <OPTION> settings.

Simply customising the existing text may be all that is necessary for some Wizard pages, though extra text and form elements can be added as required.

If you prefer to start from a blank page, you still have a decent set of tools for formatting and for inserting images, forms and tables. It's more or less WYSIWYG, and you have dialog box control over most features – though with significantly fewer options than you find in Netscape's editor.

If you are using an older version of Word, you can get an add-on from Microsoft – the Internet Assistant for Word – to give you a similar level of HTML editing facilities.

—————— 12.5 FrontPage Express ——————

FrontPage Express is supplied with Internet Explorer 4.0. It competes head-on with Composer's Editor, offering the same range of facilities and ease of use – with the extra bonus of icons for form fields (though setting up the form itself takes some skill and effort). It also offers a few WebBots – a kind of mini-program that runs when the page is uploaded to the server, or a visitor views the page.

Like the Editor, FrontPage Express cannot handle frames. It also has a few peculiarities. When you insert a new table, its BORDER WIDTH is initially 0, making it invisible and hard to work with! If you set a background image, you may also have to set the background colour to make the image visible – depending on the colours of the image. Editing tables can be awkward – if you delete the contents of a cell, the cell itself is deleted and the remaining cells shuffled round! But these are all things that you soon learn to live with, and are outweighed by the ease with which it handles routine text formatting, images and links.

FRONTPAGE

FrontPage Express is a cut-down version of FrontPage, a fully-featured Web site management system. This provides all the facilities that are needed to create and maintain a commercial intranet (internal web) or Web site.

FrontPage has two displays. The **Editor** is almost identical to that of Express, though with additional facilities – it can handle frames, and it has a larger set of WebBots. The **Explorer** window (see next page) gives an overview of the whole structure. From here you can delete, move or select pages for editing.

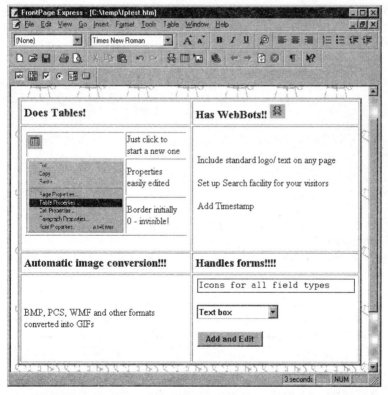

FrontPage Express has icons for everything – including form fields.

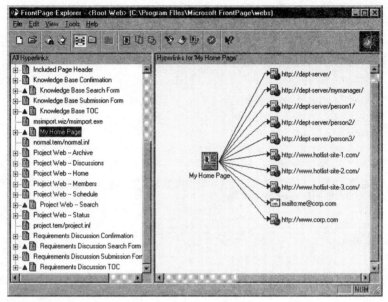

The FrontPage Explorer window, showing the links between pages.

12.6 Summary

- With CompuServe's Home Page Wizard you can easily produce sets of pages, but you are limited to simple designs, with graphics and links dropped in.

- The Netscape Editor simplifies many aspects of HTML, though it cannot handle forms or frames.

- Word 97 can produce HTML documents, though it handles only the basic text, image and links tags.

- FrontPage Express can cope with the full range of HTML tags, except those for frames.

- With FrontPage you can develop and manage a large multi-page structure.

13

HTML SUMMARY

13.1 HTML 2.0

Structure
\<HTML\> \</HTML\> Enclose the whole document
\<HEAD\> \</HEAD\> Enclose the information area
\<TITLE\>\</TITLE\> Define the name to appear in the title bar, and in browsers' Bookmarks
\<BODY\> \</BODY\> Enclose the displayed page

Headings and breaks
\<Hn\>\</Hn\> Heading at level n – 1 is largest size
\<P\> Start of Paragraph
    ALIGN = *Left / Center / Right* aligns text
\<BR\> Line Break
\<HR\> Horizontal Rule
    SIZE = *Value* in pixels
    WIDTH = *Value* in pixels or percentage
    NOSHADE Makes the line solid
\<PRE\>\</PRE\> Preformatted text; preserves line breaks
\<ADDRESS\>\</ADDRESS\> Normally holds author's address
\<!... comment ...\> Not displayed by browser

Character formats
\<B\>\</B\> **Bold**
\<I\>\</I\> *Italic*
\<TT\>\</TT\> `Typewriter`

<CITE></CITE> Citation – used for quotations
<CODE></CODE> Computer source code
<EM></EM> Emphasized = **<I>**
<KBD></KBD> Keyboard entry = **<TT>**
<SAMP></SAMP> Text sample
<STRONG></STRONG> Strongly emphasized = **<B>**
<VAR></VAR> Variable name

Lists
<UL></UL> Unordered (bulletted) List
<OL></OL> Ordered (numbered or lettered) list
<LI> List Item
<DL></DL> Definition List
<DT> Term in definition list
<DD> Definition

Links and anchors
<A HREF = *URL*>*Link*</A> Hypertext link between *Link* text
  or image and local or remote *URL*
<A NAME = *Target*>*Text*</A> Creates a jump target in a page

Images
<IMG SRC = *Image*> Displays the *Image* (GIF or JPG)
  ALT = *Text* to display if image is not downloaded
  ALIGN = *Top*/*Bottom*/*Middle* aligns following text

Forms
<FORM...></FORM> Encloses the Form area
  METHOD = *Post* (*Get*, not covered here, also possible)
  ACTION = Your e-mail address
<INPUT ...> Data entry by visitor
  NAME = *Name* of variable to store data
  SIZE = *Width* in characters
  TYPE = *Checkbox*/*Radio* options
        Reset/*Submit* buttons
        Password hides input text

\<TEXTAREA ...\> Multi-line text entry
    NAME = *Name* of variable to store data
    ROWS = *Number* of rows to display
    COLS = *Number* of columns to display
\<SELECT ...\> Sets up drop-down list
    NAME = *Name* of variable to store data
    SIZE = *Number* of items to display at one time
    MULTIPLE Allow multiple selections
\<OPTION VALUE = *RetVal*\> *ListItem* Display *ListItem* in
    Select list; pass *RetVal* to NAME variable
\</SELECT\> Closes Select list

—— 13.2 Netscape extensions ——

\<BODY ...\> options
    BACKGROUND = *Image*, repeated if space available
    BGCOLOR = *Colour value* of background
    TEXT = *Colour value* of text
    LINK = *Colour value* of unvisited links
    VLINK = *Colour value* of visited links
    ALINK = *Colour value* of active links

Text options
\<CENTER\>\</CENTER\> Centres text (or images)
\<BLINK\>\</BLINK\> Flashing text
\<FONT ...\>\</FONT\> Encloses text to be formatted with..
    SIZE = *Number*, 1 to 7 (largest) for size of text
    COLOR = *Colour value* of following text

———— 13.3 HTML 3.0 ————

\<SUP\>\</SUP\> Superscript
\<SUB\>\</SUB\> Subscript

<IMG SRC> options

WIDTH = *Value* in pixels or percentage of window width
HEIGHT = *Value* in pixels or percentage of window height

Tables

<TABLE ...></TABLE> Encloses Table code
  BORDER = *Width* of border; narrow if no *width* given;
  CELLSPACING = *Value* in pixels of distance between inner and outer borders
  CELLPADDING = *Value* in pixels of distance between inner border and text

<CAPTION ...></CAPTION> Encloses text of caption
  ALIGN = *Top / Bottom* – default to *Top*

<TR></TR> Encloses a row

<TH ...></TH> Enclose a row or column header cell

<TD ...></TD> Enclose a data cell
  COLSPAN = *Number* of columns to spread cell across
  ROWSPAN = *Number* of rows to stretch cell down
  ALIGN = *Left / Right / Center* horizontal alignment of item in header or data cell
  VALIGN = *Top / Middle / Bottom* vertical alignment
  WIDTH = *Value* in pixels for width of cell

───────── **13.4 Netscape 2.0** ─────────

Frames

<FRAMESET ...> Start of frame section, in layout document and replacing the normal BODY elements. The tag must contain either a ROWS or COLS option.
  ROWS = Divides the window into frames horizontally, specifying the size of each either in pixels, or as a percentage of the space, or using '*' to share remaining space.
  COLS = Divides the window into frames vertically, specifying sizes as above.

</FRAMESET> End of frame section

<FRAME ...> Defines the content and nature of a frame
  SRC = URL of document
  NAME = Name of frame, if to be used as TARGET of HREF link
  SCROLLING = *Yes / No / Auto* – controls appearance of scroll bars around frame
  NORESIZE Forces fixed size frame.
<NOFRAMES></NOFRAMES> Encloses code to be displayed in browsers which cannot handle frames.
  TARGET = *Name / _self / _parent / _top / _blank* – HREF option to specify where a document is to be displayed.

––––––––––––– **13.5 HTML 3.2** –––––––––––––

This incorporates the Netscape 2.0 extensions and adds some new tags. To conform to the specification, a document should start with a DOCTYPE tag, identifying it as version 3.2:

<!DOCTYPE HTML PUBLIC "-//W3C//DTD HTML 3.2//EN">

It should also contain a TITLE. Other new tags include:

<ISINDEX> Defines phrase for keyword searches.
<BASE HREF = ...> Sets the base URL. Use it where files are stored in a set of folders and sub-folders.
<SCRIPT> Used with JavaScript and other scripting languages.
<STYLE> For future use with style sheets – planned for HTML 4.0.
<META> Used to carry the author's name, search keywords and other information.
<APPLET ...> Defines a Java applet

──── ON-LINE RESOURCES ────

Submit It! The one-stop approach to advertising your page
http://www.submit-it.com

Babel Glossary of acronyms and abbreviations.
http://www.access.digex.net/~ikind/babel96a.html

Carl Davis's HTML Editor Reviews Reviews of all the commercial and shareware HTML editors with links to their suppliers' sites.
http://homepage.interaccess.com/~cdavis/edit_rev.html

HTML Editors Software and links to more software
http://www.utoronto.ca/webdocs/HTMLdocs/PCTOOLS/
    pc_editors.html

Java Boutique Start here if you want to explore Java
http://javaboutique.internet.com/

Netscape's JavaScript Guide If you are using Netscape, just open the Help menu and select Handbook while you are on-line. The Guide is reached from the first page.

MapEdit Software for easy image map creation
http://www.boutell.com/index.html

Web Tools Go here to add a counter to your page
http://www.webtools.org/counter

Teach Yourself HTML Examples and links
http://www.tcp.co.uk/~macbride/tybooks.htm

Shareware Central An excellent place to find shareware.
http://www.shareware.com

Yahoo The best of the Internet directories – you can find almost everything from here.
http://www.yahoo.com

INDEX

Symbols

.HTM extension 87
.HTML extension 21, 87
40, 77
<!Comments> 31
</MAP> 179
<A HREF ...> 68, 168
<A NAME = 73
<ADDRESS> 23
<APPLET > 193
<AREA ...> 178
<B> 32
<BLINK> 33
<BODY> 24

 25
<CAPTION > 147
<CENTER> 48
<DD> 113
<DL> 113
<DT> 113
<EMPHASIS> 32
<FONT COLOR = 37
<FONT SIZE = value> 28
<FORM ...> 124
<FRAME SRC = ... > 164
<FRAMESET ...> 162
<H1> 18
<HEAD> 24
<HR> 25
<I> 32
<IMG SRC = > 44
<INPUT> 124, 128
<ISINDEX> 101
<LI> 106
<MAP NAME = ...> 177
<META> 101

<NOFRAMES> 166
<OL> 110
<OPTION = ...> 131
<P> 25
<PARAM> 194
<PRE> 35
<SELECT ...> 131
<STRONG> 32
<SUB> 34
<SUP> 34
<TABLE> 142
<TD> 142
<TEXTAREA ...> 130
<TH> 147
<TITLE> 23
<TR> 142
<TT> 32
<UL> 106

A

Addresses, for links 69
ALIGN 30
   HR option 118
   TH / TD option 152
   with graphics 46
Aligning text 30
Alignment, in tables 152
ALT, IMG SRC option 78
Analysing returns 136
Anchor tag 67, 73
Angle brackets 2, 19
Animated GIFs 187
Applets 11, 193

B

BACKGROUND, BODY option
   55